J. H. H St. John

Pakeha Rambles Through Maori Lands

J. H. H St. John

Pakeha Rambles Through Maori Lands

ISBN/EAN: 9783744743617

Printed in Europe, USA, Canada, Australia, Japan

Cover: Foto ©ninafisch / pixelio.de

More available books at **www.hansebooks.com**

Sketch Map
— shewing portion of the —
NORTH ISLAND OF
NEW ZEALAND

East C.

BAY OF PLENTY

THAMES

'KLAND

MERCER

Waikato R.

TAURANGA

MAKETU
WHAKATANE
OHIWA
OPOTIKI

NEWCASTLE

HAMILTON

ROTOITI
ROTORUA

URIWERA COUNTRY

GISBORNE

ORMOND

CAMBRIDGE

TARAWERA
ROTOMAHANA

WAIKARE
MTS

TE REINGA

Poverty
Bay

ALEXANDRA

Waipa R.

WAIRAU
MOANA

CLYDE

Mohaka R.

TAPUAEHARURU

TAUPO L.

Hawke's
Bay

KAIMANAWA
RANGE

HAPIER

Tongariro
Ruapehu

PAKEHA RAMBLES

THROUGH MAORI LANDS.

BY

LIEUT.-COLONEL ST. JOHN

(NEW ZEALAND MILITIA).

WELLINGTON:
PRINTED BY ROBERT BURRETT, MOLESWORTH STREET.
1873.

PREFACE.

Some explanation is due why a description of "Waikato Forty Years Ago" appears in a book professedly written by a colonist of only ten years standing. The facts are these : a valued friend kindly gave me a MSS. containing his early experiences in New Zealand, with the proviso that, in case of publication, his name should not appear ; I had to respect his wishes, and I have consequently assumed a degree of authorship to which I am not entitled, reserving to myself the right of confession.

For the more modern portion I am solely responsible.

I have only to add that my "Rambles" were not always as consecutive as I have described them ; for the sake of convenience I have connected together numerous journeys made at various intervals.

J. H. H. St. J.

Wellington, 20th August, 1873.

ERRATA.

In page xvii, lines 7 and 20, *for* " Heke" *read* " Hika."

In pages 172, 180, 188, and 196, head-line, *for* " Pehaka" *read* " Pakeha."

PART I.

Waikato Forty Years Ago.

My reminiscences of Waikato date from my arrival on the 10th November 1830. I had been at Sydney for some time, and made up my mind to try the New Zealand trade; so I took my passage on board the brigantine "Sydney Packet," and found three other passengers, Mr. S. Paul (who was part owner), and two Waikato chiefs, Te Karekare, and Te Puia; these latter had been taken for a trip to Sydney, but were in reality hostages. The approach to the coast was predicted, before land was sighted, by a strong-nosed sailor, who swore he could smell the peculiar fragrance of the New Zealand soil, &c. Four hours after Jack's assertion, land was seen, but I never could manage to train my olfactory nerves to such perfection.

We were not acquainted with the mouth of the Waikato River, and so we got a boat into a little nook to the southward of the bar, and brought off Captain Payne, a resident trader, who gave us the benefit of his experience; with his help we got safely over, and anchored opposite **Te Rori a Karihi.** On going ashore we, the new arrivals (*nga pakeha hou*), were introduced to the assembled chiefs, who also gave a grand reception to our dark skinned fellow passengers: there was feeding on a large scale; and, to my

B

great astonishment, crying to any extent. It is a queer
thing, this *tangi*. Whether it was a funeral, or a meeting
of friends after an absence, the tears flowed copiously.
Even in these degenerate days, this twenty-female-weeping
power has not entirely deserted the race; but they don't
cry like they used when I first came to New Zealand.

The news of our arrival soon spread inland, and lots more
people came to see the vessel (*kaipuke*). The electric telegraph does beat the Maoris in the diffusion of intelligence,
but I think they need not give in to anything else; they
lick the semaphores into fits. Given a piece of news, a
young native, and a screwy pony, and it is quite marvellous
to trace how speedily all *kaingas* around learn what it is all
about. Naturally, the communication being verbal, there
is a good deal of exaggeration; but still, news do travel fast
in Maoridom. Of course the new comers went in for their
share of *tangi* and *kai*.

Te Karekare was a middle-aged man with a family, and
was about the best disposed New Zealander I have ever
come across; on the passage down I struck up an intimacy
with him, which I am happy to say continued without
a break to the day of his death, which occurred at the
Ihutaroa fight many years afterwards; and on more than
one occasion I received many kindnesses from him. After
having been ashore a short time, we took a trip up the
country to Toroakapakapa, a settlement a considerable
distance up the Waipa River, a branch of the Waikato.
On our way up we stopped to breakfast, preparing it on the
ground near the water's edge: our party being large, and
occupying about a dozen canoes, took up some distance
along the bank. Our chief, Piraoa, intending to introduce
his *pakehas* in a grand and becoming style, had enlisted a
large number of the *élite* to accompany him; and the party
of Europeans consisted of Captain Payne, Logan (the man

servant), and myself. It being summer time, and the weather particularly fine, many during the halt were in the water bathing, whilst breakfast was preparing; and amongst the bathers was Logan. After he had been in the river a short time a commotion arose amongst those on shore; seeing several men rush into the water with tomahawks, and imagining they were about to kill him, he cried out at the top of his voice " Piraoa, Piraoa, de natif make a bunga bunga me;" this he kept on repeating, and was nearly drowned in his fright; it was some time before we could pacify him by explaining that the native's rush was in consequence of some dogs on the opposite side of the river having caught a pig, which was heard squealing most lustily, and which they were swimming across to secure, without waiting to unfasten their canoes. We were the first Europeans, barring one, who had been in that part of New Zealand. I forget the man's name; but he had come from Kawhia, from a vessel in that port (I heard that he was her mate), with the intention of proceeding across the country to the Thames. On his arriving at Te Onematua, the settlement of the Ngatipou, Te Uira, the elder son of Taratikitiki, the principal chief of the tribe, hearing of his intended trip, endeavoured to delay his departure for a few days, as he purposed going that way himself, in order that he might be in company and under protection. The man, however, persisted in setting out, and Te Uira directed some slaves to take care of him. They started, and a short time afterwards returned without the *pakeha*. According to their statement, which is very doubtful, a misunderstanding arose from the *pakeha* having threatened to strike one of them; their report was that when halted to prepare food on the bank of the River Waipa on their way down, and when he (still maintaining his threatening attitude) stepped ashore, they had paddled the canoe away, taking his clothing

and food, and leaving him on the bank by himself. He
was subsequently discovered by a party of another tribe,
naked and dead, buoyed up by a limb of a tree at the
water's edge: the river having subsided had no doubt left
him in that position a few miles below where he had been
marooned. There were no marks of violence further than
slight abrasions occasioned by the body floating along the
bed of the river when carried down by the current, and it
was supposed that he had been drowned, probably in the
attempt to cross some of the tributary creeks. This having
occurred a short time previously to our arrival, was the
principal topic of conversation, and every endeavour was
made to exculpate the chiefs from any participation in so
unwarrantable an act; in fact, Te Uira was so much
incensed with the party that, had they not made themselves
scarce, he would in all probability have had them shot. One
only of them again made his appearance, and that not till
after a lapse of time. The natives, generally, were very
indignant at the occurrence, considering that they would
be stigmatized as a body. On the passage up the river we
had an opportunity of seeing a considerable collection of
natives at the different settlements, our visit being anticipated from fore-runners having gone ahead to trumpet our
chief's success in having secured several *Atuas* (spirits) in the
flesh, some of whom he was about exhibiting for their
wonderment and admiration. At all the settlements we
were received most courteously and hospitably, though the
younger portions of the community generally hid behind
stumps of trees, in, or behind, houses, or under the garments
of the elder portion, occasionally stealing a peep at "*Te
Atua.*"

At one settlement, Kopokowhatitiri, where we stopped for
the night, we saw the natives go through a dance; they
mustered nearly a hundred, and stood out in separate files,

the men apart from the women, about fifty in each row : the men, generally speaking, young and robust, the women from about 15 years to 25, and some of them good looking ; each party of course dressed entirely in their native habiliments. The Maoris in former days were much finer men than they are at present ; they now speak of themselves as having been a people of large stature, which is borne out by the discovery of their remains. The day of our arrival at Toroakapakapa, I perceived a great commotion in the village, the men arming and demanding arms from us, the women rushing about in all directions, and the clatter of tongues representing a modern " Babel." There **was** a party of natives at a short distance on the opposite side of a gully, and my want of knowledge of the language immediately led me to the conclusion that these strangers were a hostile party about to make a raid on the settlement and on ourselves : consequently I armed myself after the approved manner of New Zealand, with a well-filled cartridge box strapped round my waist, and, musket in hand, was preparing myself for a good shot at the supposed enemy. Selecting for my mark a fine fellow, who was sitting out in front of his party unconscious of any intended ill, either for himself or his people, I was going to let drive when, to my surprise, I was seized from behind and prevented from firing : by dint of perseverance on the part of the natives, I was made to understand that this was a friendly visit of some relatives who had come to see the *pakehas,* and that I was aiming at a friend. From the action I had taken I gained the credit of being a resolute and determined warrior, which I believe I have retained ever since ; not that I was at all pugnacious, but I **always** bore in mind the adage " That caution is the better part of valour," and I was very careful not to encounter men of superior strength to myself in the few wrestles I had for amusement ; I accepted the challenge only of those whom I

considered inferior to myself in strength, and declined a
second round after having succeeded in throwing my adversary in the first instance, which I usually did. I only lost
the first throw in one case out of two, which were the sole
occasions of *riri* (earnest) I had with the natives. We remained at Toroakapakapa a week, as Captain Payne's object
in going up the river was to purchase flax to freight the
"Sydney Packet" back to Sydney; I had thus an opportunity of seeing occasionally a large assemblage of natives,
but I had daily to go through the same routine, endeavouring to learn Maori by day, and watching the dancing and
games of the natives in the evening. We found a difference
on going back, for the passage which had occupied a week
when ascending the river, took us only two days on our
return. There was now collected a good amount of flax as
a cargo for the vessel ; but, as still more was required to fill
up and dispatch her, the mate (Tucker) was sent along the
coast to look after some which the natives had cleaned : on
his return with it by sea, the canoe which carried him and
his flax was swamped, and he was drowned. The natives
who accompanied him were saved, but the flax and the canoe
were lost. I believe he had been cautioned not to go to sea
in the canoe.

An incident occurred about this time, showing one way
of securing a friend. I was carrying three damaged
muskets to send off to Sydney for repairs, and a chief
named Nini (who from his wild and turbulent spirit was
nicknamed by us "Russian") requested leave to look at
them : as they were defective, it was desirable that they
should not be seen, so I objected ; he thereupon seized hold
of one of them, and, to retain possession of it, I had to drop
the others, but the natives around did not attempt to touch
them as they lay on the ground. There was a struggle for
the mastery, and after a time I contrived to manœuvre him

to the edge of a bank about 8 feet in height, and there I succeeded in placing my foot on his chest, and wrenching the piece out of his hands. My friend, of course, went down the bank, and fell amongst the boulders on the beach; on his recovering himself he jumped up, foaming at the mouth, and danced about with rage for about twenty minutes, swearing vengeance on account of his defeat. This was at least my impression, as at that time I did not know anything of the language; after this explosion he took himself off.

The next day as I was wandering about the place where I had had the squabble I happened to look up, and I saw Nini approaching, accompanied by ten or twelve other natives. It would never have done for a *pakeha* to show the white feather, although I fully expected a combined attack, so I stood my ground. Nini advanced towards me, holding out his hand in *pakeha* fashion, but this I at first declined to take, thinking that he might by retaining my hand, have me at a great disadvantage; and it was not till after some time that his companions contrived to make me understand his intentions were particularly friendly, upon which I gave him my hand at once, and I am happy to say I retained his unbroken friendship up to the fight of Te Ihutaroa, the last intertribal war that took place among the Maoris in Waikato, when Nini went down with many others. I received many kindnesses from him, as well as protection from the importunities of other Maoris, though I was not supposed to be living under his wing, or that of his tribe; and I always found him particularly honourable and generous.

In 1831, the brig "Tranmere," Captain Smith, arrived in Manakau Harbour with Captain Kent, Te Wherowhero, and Amohia, Wherowhero's daughter. Captain Kent was the first European who had visited the West Coast of the

North Island for trading purposes, having put in to Kawhia, in 1828, in the brig "Macquarie," for flax, that being the only article of commerce produced by the natives. In consequence of Te Wherowhero's visiting Manukau with his *pakehas* (*pakehas* in those days were no small beer, and as I have said before were looked upon more in the light of Celestials, or, as the natives would term it, *Atuas*), Te Kanae Wetere presented Te Wherowhero with Awhitu, a pretty little bay to the south, a little inside of the entrance to the Manukau Harbour; in return for this Wetere received the gift of a case of muskets, considerably above the value of the land: but in those days the chiefs used to endeavour to excel each other in the value and magnificence of their presents. Awhitu has since been considered as the property of the Ngatimahuta (Te Wherowhero's tribe), and Honana te Maioha received a piece of it as compensation for his claim as a Ngatimahuta, on the confiscation of the Waikato lands by the Government. Captain Kent, Te Wherowhero, his daughter Amohia, and an escort of natives came over to the Waikato, and proceeded up the river. Whilst they were in Manukau I paid a visit to the "Tranmere" to see Captain Smith, going in company with some natives by way of Waiuku. On crossing over to the portage we fell in with an old woman, left behind by a party of the Ngatipaou, which had preceded us a couple of days, and as we could not take her on we also had to leave her, with the intention of picking her up on our return. In the absence of a canoe we had to tramp along the margin of the bays, crossing, when possible, the mud flats to shorten the distance; once I ventured too far out, and got so bogged in the stiff salt water mud, that I had to be pulled out by flax ropes; at last, by dint of perseverance, with legs cut and scratched by the shells in the mud, exhausted and fatigued, we contrived to get abreast of the vessel and hail her, and to

my great relief made myself heard, and was taken on board.
I was received most kindly, and remained on board three
days to recover myself. After obtaining a few supplies from
Captain Smith, we were taken up to Waiuku in the ship's
boat, thus probably escaping a second bogging and dragging
out; and on our way we found the old lady where we had left
her, and took her on; by the time we reached Waiuku it
was evening, and we crossed over the portage to Purapura.
The night promised to be fine, and so we did not trouble
ourselves to erect a shed, but presently the wind shifted and
the rain fell in torrents; it was now pitch dark, and there
was no alternative but to sit up, grin, and bear it; the
water was literally running through me. At day light the
natives contrived to make a break-wind, so that we could
relieve ourselves of our wet clothing, not that my companions had much to wet: the principal mode they adopted
was to turn their mats in and out, and out and in, till they
were dry. The old lady we had picked up was taken poses-
sion of by our chief Piraoa, who was with us, as a stray
waif, and was walked off to the settlement. Soon after this
Piraoa's wife was confined, and the old lady was deputed to
attend upon her; the consequence being that she was *tapued*
(or rendered sacred), the chieftainess in the straw being a
woman of rank. At the time of the occurrence food was
very scarce; there was only fern root, and of this the best
was selected for the chiefs; the old woman being a slave
was, during the time of the *tapu*, precluded from feeding
herself; but on one occasion no one being there to cook for her
and feed her, she unceremoniously, but unfortunately, appropriated some of the sacred fern root meant for the chieftainess,
and made a hearty meal. Detection followed; not even a
form of trial was gone through, and the poor old thing was
killed, and sunk in the river during the night. In the
morning we saw some blood on the ground, but were told on

c

enquiry that it was the blood of a dog; we then missed the old woman, but were informed that she had been sent up the river.

One evening the "Sydney Packet," being full, took her departure for Sydney, and at day-light next morning I ascended a hill, expecting to find that she had got out of sight, or was merely a speck in the off'ng. To my surprise I discovered that she was ashore on the north side; on going out she had gone too far to the north, had struck, and was thrown up where she was then lying. On striking she had carried away her rudder, become unmanageable, and been buffetted about till she reached high water mark, where the tide left her. Captain Payne and the rest of us went across to render what assistance we could; we lightened the vessel by landing her cargo, stores, and all rigging not essentially required for the vessel's use, and at the top of the next spring tide, which occurred in about ten days, we succeeded in getting her afloat and inside the harbour again.

At a subsequent period the "Elizabeth and Mary," a vessel of about 90 tons, the same size as the "Sydney Packet," got on shore at the same place, but with worse luck, as she stuck and became a total wreck : no life in either case was lost or endangered.

We repaired the damage done to the "Sydney Packet," re-loaded her, and dispatched her to Sydney, where she arrived in safety without any more troubles.

On the departure of the vessel we commenced operations to secure a cargo for her return, which we calculated would be in about six weeks, or two months; but she never made her appearance, and the "Samuel," a schooner, came in her place. During the absence of the vessel we had wars and rumours of wars up the country among the natives. The fights in Waikato have been pretty numerous, whether they arose from the attacks of an invading foe, or from local squabbles ; and it may not be out of place if I give a short account of some of them, beginning at the attack by the Ngapuhis in 1825 or 1826 on Waikato, before the tribes inhabiting the latter were supplied with fire arms. The raid was made by Hongi Hika, at the head of 800 men, after his visit to England, where he had been presented with a suit of armour and some fire arms by George IV. ; these he carried with him, and used in the expedition. The Waikatos at the time of the above raid were in possession of none but their native arms. Notwithstanding this disadvantage they made a stand at Matakitaki, where they had built a pa just at the confluence of the Mangapiko stream with the Waipa River. Ngapuhi made the attack on the pa early on a foggy morning. On the report of the fire arms the besieged were paralysed with astonishment and fear ; they could not tell whence these extraordinary sounds proceeded, and many were shot down without a semblance of resistance.

The Waikatos in fortifying their pa had intersected it with *Maioros* (or rifle pits), and in the rush they made to escape hundreds fell, or were driven into these, and trampled to death or smothered. A great slaughter of the Waikatos was the consequence, the estimated loss being 2,000 killed (and eaten), and 2,000 taken away prisoners. Many of the principal chiefs, both male and female, were killed or taken, though several contrived to escape from their captors on the road, and return to their homes. Potatau's chief wife, and Te Uira's were among the captured who managed to get away. One of the leading chiefs of the Ngapuhi connived at the escape of a "rangatira" Waikato woman with her son. She, it seems, had fallen to the lot of a man of inferior rank, and one of the Ngapuhi happening to pass by recognised her as a person from whom he had received hospitality and kindness on a previous visit to Waikato, and

tried to obtain her liberty from her present master. Failing
in this, he determined to effect her deliverance by cautioning
the owner to look well after his prisoners, as probably they
might attempt to escape. He threw him off his guard, and
gained his confidence to such an extent that his offer to
assist in the watch was gladly received and accepted. The
house in which the prisoners were confined was fortunately
at the edge of the high bank of the Waipa River. After
collecting a number of sticks, which had the appearance of
being for firewood, the friendly chief excavated from the
bank into the house, and having made a good passage, he
covered the aperture in the whare with the wood and with
fern. In the middle of the night, when all were supposed to
be asleep, the sticks were moved aside, the woman and child
passed through the aperture, and got to the river unheard ;
this the woman swam with the child on her back, and
eventually both reached her friends in safety. To favour
their escape the kindly native, after their exit by the
passage, replaced the sticks and fern, and made up their
bedding as if they were there asleep. Their lord and
master was sleeping in the house with them, and it was not
till after daylight that he discovered the deception that had
been practised on him, to the great amusement of the others.

One of the principal chieftains, Te Rangimoewaka, had
succeeded in escaping from the pa, but becoming exhausted
with fatigue he sat down, telling the party with whom he
was escaping to hasten away and not heed him, as he could
proceed no further. For a time there was some hesitation,
but the yells of the pursuers grew nearer and nearer, and
the instinct of self-preservation carried the day : each gave
him the final salute by applying nose to nose, and hastened
off. Amongst the pursuers was a Ngapuhi chief, who knew
Te Rangimoewaka, and had been on friendly terms with
him. He was the first to come up ; and, seeing his quondam

friend lying exhausted, reminiscences of old times flashed across him; he stooped and rubbed noses in token of recognition; and then, in performance of his duty to his party, tomahawked him.

Success is not always a good thing: **it makes** some people conceited, and only leads them to a fall; and this is precisely what happened to Ngapuhi. Heke's expedition had been attended with glorious results, and they did not see **why** such good fortune should not continue. So, after a lapse of two or three years, Ngapuhi got up another war-party **to** the Waikato, without calculating the advance in *civilization* the Waikatos had made in the interim; for, warned by their defeat of the superiority of fire arms, they had **made** wonderful efforts to get supplied with arms and ammunition. Pomare, Moetara, and several chiefs of importance, with others amounting **in** all to **about five** hundred men, formed the *taua* (a war party). When the Ngapuhis entered the Waikato country the inhabitants retired from the banks of the river, permitting the enemy to advance unmolested. The elated invaders passed the spot of Hongi Heke's victory, and marched on some two or three miles further, without seeing a foe. At the Mangauika rapids, near Kopua, close to the place where a mission was afterwards established, they came into collision with the Waikatos; and, to their disgust, found them in strong numbers, well posted, and well armed. There was no more easy slaughtering fun, so Ngapuhi concluded to retire. But the Waikatos had not enticed them so far up the river for nothing, and in rear of the attacking party ambushes were carefully laid on the banks of the Waipa. At Te Rore, about four miles below Alexandra (the old Matakitaki), there was assembled a large party of Ngatiteata, Ngatitipa, Ngatimahanga, and other Waikato tribes, and into this ambuscade Ngapuhi unconsciously fell. They were paddling down quietly, all the canoes close together, when a heavy

volley was poured into them. Orders had been given to
take special aim at the chiefs, and most of them, Pomare
included, fell at the first fire. The canoes jammed and upset.
There was no climbing up the banks under the heavy fire,
and volley after volley came hurtling from the concealed
Waikatos. Ngapuhi were, of course, totally defeated, and
those who managed to escape got out on the left bank and
made for Whangaroa, where they got another cutting up.
The survivors then pushed on overland for Waikato Heads;
but in the meantime the Waikato canoes had carried a large
party to cut off the retreat. This was done so effectually
that, out of the five hundred, or more, men who composed
the *taua*, only ten reached their homes, Moetara being the
only chief who did so; and he had been struck by a spent
ball on the chest, where had been pricked a star to which
he attributed his invulnerability.

In 1830, Kaipaka, a pa near Otawhao, occupied by the
Ngatihinetu and Ngatiapakura, was attacked by the Ngatihauas, Ngatikoroki, and Ngatiruru, who perpetrated an indiscriminate slaughter of men, women, and children. The
following anecdote was related to me by a woman who belonged to the assaulting party. She had saved from drowning an infant that had been thrown into the creek (Mangapiko) which ran close to the pa. On taking it from the water
she had nestled it to her bosom to warm it and preserve its
life if possible; the poor little thing unfortunately uttered a
cry; a savage passing by heard it, and he immediately
seized the child, tore it from her, notwithstanding her re-
monstrances, and deliberately stuck it up before the fire and
roasted it alive.

Another local fight took place, in 1830, at Te Whakakiho,
a pa occupied by the Ngatipou. The majority of its inhabitants being away at Kawhia and elsewhere, the opportunity to take it was too good to be lost, and it was attacked

by surprise (*he konihi*) by the Ngatihaua, Ngatikoroki, and Ngatimahuta. Heavy loss of life occurred here also ; but the intervention of the pakehas so completely pacified the belligerents that the conquered party did not, as usual in such cases, seek *utu* (payment) when they became strong enough to do so.

In 1831, Te Haowhenua, Taumatawiwi, and other encounters took place between the Hauraki tribes and the Ngatihauas, etc., in alliance with others of the Waikato tribes. From these arose the famous "Aroha" case, which has given so much trouble in the Native Lands Court. The struggle between the two tribes took place in 1831, and ended in the expulsion of the Hauraki (Thames natives), who did not attempt to recover their lands till after the Native Lands Court was instituted and the discovery was made that the country was auriferous.

The last war expedition of the Ngapuhis to the Waikato was made in the autumn of 1832. On the intimation of an intended attack, the Waikatos mustered their various tribes to the extent of 3,000, or more, fighting men, the greater portion bearing firearms. They assembled near Waikato Heads, and showed so strong that the Ngapuhi scouts on the other side of the river advised the main body to halt. A party of our people, who had crossed over, came upon the footprints of their advance guard, and Waikato at once turned out for leaping parade. There were about three thousand of them, and their war dance, in fighting costume, was something terrific; the simultaneous thump of six thousand feet striking the earth in spring after spring, and all in perfect unison, made the earth literally shake. We could feel it as they came down from the upward leaps. The disadvantage of such numbers was that the enemy would not come on, and that the commissariat department was not up to feeding so many very hungry mouths. Of course had Ngapuhi made the attack, there would have been plenty to eat; but they fought shy, trusting perhaps to the very circumstances which did happen. For, after a few days had passed, the Waikatos found they had eaten up everything about the place, and that they could no longer remain. It was thought better that the Europeans should accompany their retreat, so Captain Payne, myself, and my servant went with them. Mr. W——, of Onewhero, a man called "Cooper," from his trade, and a half-caste New Holland lad preferred to stay, little anticipating the fate in store for them.

About a month after we had left our establishment, the Ngapuhis made their appearance at Putataka, where I had resided, burned my house, and killed the stock I had running there. They also captured Cooper and "Billy boy," the New Holland half-caste, and took them away, at the same time stripping and burning their dwelling. They then went up the river to Onewhero, seized Mr. W—— at daybreak, and killed several natives. One lad managed to escape into the river, where he lay concealed for hours with only his nose and mouth above water, till the *taua* had returned. At the capture of Mr. W——, an altercation took place between two chiefs, Pukerangi and another (whose name has escaped my memory), as to the proprietorship of the captive. Pukerangi persisted in his claim by right of priority, as he had been the first to enter the room in which W—— was, and, moreover, had seized him before the other had entered. Pukerangi's claim was approved of by the other chiefs, and they proceeded up the river about forty miles to Whangape Lake, where they surprised and massacred between 40 and 50 men. The slaughter would have been more serious had not a canoe full of the Waikatos been fortunately going down the river, and met the invading party coming up. The Waikato natives discovered their dilemma in time, turned and retreated, but were fired upon by the advancing Ngapuhis; they returned the fire, and a running fight ensued. The Ngapuhis succeeded in killing one of the Waikatos, but in return a chief was shot and fell into the water. The recovery of the body occasioned considerable delay, which was of signal advantage to the retreating party, as it gave them an opportunity of disposing of the dead man that was in their canoe by placing him ashore, and thus lightening their load, and of apprizing others who would otherwise have been surprised and probably massacred or captured. On the Ngapuhi reaching Whangape they stopped in the creek, the entrance to the lake; and during the night a canoe with a large party of the Waikatos in it pulled through the midst of the war party, which had lined each side of the creek. When challenged, they succeeded in imitating so well the Ngapuhi dialect that they were believed to be some of the attacking party, and got clear. On their return, the Ngapuhi revisited Port Waikato, and fell in with a pakeha known by the name of " Paddy," who had travelled from Whaingaroa (Raglan); they wished to take him away with them, and probably might not have seriously ill-treated him, but Paddy, imagining that they were Waikato natives, and probably not having heard of the Ngapuhi's arrival, declined the honor and became obstreperous. The consequence was that he was killed, and an endeavour made to turn him to a useful account by cooking him; but, on being placed on the festive ground (board being out of the question), he was found to be so much impregnated with salt from the salt provision he had eaten, that he was rejected, and ultimately given to the dogs.

The natives were very different in those days to what they are now. They could hardly be induced to touch salt or salt provision. Paddy got no more than his deserts though; he was an incorrigibly bad character, having robbed all the Europeans at Whaingaroa; his last act was the robbing of some natives with whom he had been living and from

whom he had to decamp, and thus rush upon his fate. I had
nearly shared the same fate; as, imagining from the length
of time which had elapsed without any appearance of the
enemy, that it was a false alarm, I had prepared for my
return to my former station; but I was delayed by bad
weather. Had it not been for this, I should have been just
in time to be caught; as it was, I was in my canoe, on the
eve of starting, when the escaped natives gave the alarm.
Of course I returned ashore, thanking my stars at my
narrow escape. On its being known that the Ngapuhis had
arrived, killed several natives, captured the pakehas and
burned their dwellings, the Kaitutai, or Ngatiamaru, tribe
mustered and went in pursuit; but, bearing in mind the sage
saying that "discretion is the better part of valour," and
seeing the enemy too numerous when overtaken in Manakau,
they returned. The Ngatiteata, Ngatitamaho, Ngatiwhatua,
Ngatitipa, and Ngatimahanga, on hearing that the others
had come back without effecting anything, determined to
follow up the matter. They mustered immediately, and
starting without delay, followed Ngapuhi to Tawatawhiti, in
Whangarei. Here they attacked and took a pa in which
they had assembled, nearly annihilating the occupants, without the loss of a single man on their own side, and recovered
several of their own people who had been taken away from
Waikato. At the time of the mustering of the Ngatiteata,
Ngatitamaho, etc., to follow the Ngapuhis I overheard a tall,
robust slave woman say to another who was standing by her
side, looking at the natives going through their war dances
previous to departure, that as soon as they were gone she
would run away. Foolishly enough she did not wait till they
had gone, but made the attempt too soon, was captured,
and killed as an offering to propitiate the *Atua*. I was
living in the pa at the time, and hearing that they were about
to kill a slave, I seized a musket and ran with it, intending

to give it for her and save her life; but upon reaching the place, I perceived that she was breathing her last and being dragged away by the heels like a dog. Te Kanae, her chief, had struck her on the back of the neck with a tomahawk, but she was finished by some male slaves, who had smashed her face in with clubs; and these were the very men who had been on the closest terms of intimacy with the poor unfortunate woman; her name was Punepune. A short time after this, on the same day, another alarm was given that they were about killing another slave—this time, a man. I rushed off again with my gun with the same purpose as before, but on my reaching the part of the pa where they were, I was horrified to see the natives jumping about literally mad. They had surrounded the unhappy man, some were tearing out his hair by handsful, and others, unable to get close, were endeavouring to prod him with their gun muzzles. Their fiendish gestures, excited state, their thirst for blood, and the passion they had worked themselves up to was horrifying in the extreme. The poor fellow on whom they were venting their cruelty had been living with them for a length of time previously, and was on terms of intimacy with them, but, being a slave, and there being no associations connected with him, and, moreover, as he had given umbrage by an attempt to escape, he had become a subject on which they might sharpen their appetite or longing for human flesh prior to starting on the war expedition they were about undertaking. During the uproar a chief named Hika sat silently looking on, perhaps pleased with the ruthlessness of his people, and thinking probably that he might do a little business on his own account and appropriate the slave to his own use. The man was then apparently dead but possibly might recover, so Hika *tapued* him by calling him after his *iwi tuaru* (backbone), upon which he was let go, fell as dead, and remained apparently so for some time;

after a while he recovered himself sufficiently to crawl away, but it was long before he entirely recovered from the mauling he had had. The proprietor did not attempt to dispossess Hika of the slave he had thus acquired.

A few nights after our war-party had left, an old woman professed to have been visited by her *Atua*, from whom she had learnt the progress of the expedition, and getting on the roof of a house in the dark, she addressed the people of the pa, who, upon hearing her, made a fire to illuminate her. She went through the most hideous and extraordinary gesticulations whilst relating the information she had received from her *Atua*. When she was about the middle of her performance, I went stealthily and unperceived by anyone but my own party, (who, by-the-bye, were very much frightened lest the old lady might hear of it and bewitch me), to the end of the house on which she was perched, protruded my head a little above the roof, and repeated the name of the slaughtered woman, Punepune, two or three times in a slow sepulchral voice. This frightened the old Jezebel so much that in her alarm and attempt to descend from the roof of the house, she rolled off on to the ground like "a thousand of bricks." There she lay without a move, her head covered for a short time, the others supposing she had been killed by the fall; but to their surprise she became reanimated, got up on her hands and knees, and crawled away into a house on "all fours," stowing herself away in a corner until morning. Even then she continued the farce of the night before, stating that Punepune had appeared to her informing her of the proceedings of the departed expedition : in fact, she told them that she had been called from the top of the house by the dead woman, with whom she had afterwards been in communication during the night, and her revelations she would make known at a future period. That portion which she did relate did not tally with the statements made on the return of the expedition, and I never heard of her having had any further spiritual communications.

The Europeans and half-caste New Hollander captured at Port Waikato by the Ngapuhi had been taken to Whangarei where Mr. W—— was sold to his brother, who, fortunately, was there with his vessel in the harbour. On Mr. W——'s arrival, Pomare obtained him for a 25lb. keg of gunpowder from Pukerangi, and sold him to the brother for a 50lb. keg, making a cent. per cent. profit. The saying that a man's life is often dependent on a straw was verified in the case of Mr. W—— during his sojourn with his captors. As before stated, there was a disagreement between Pukerangi and another chief as to his ownership. Pukerangi treated his prisoner very fairly, having bought from some of the party a portion of W——'s wearing apparel and returned it to him, but the other fellow was in a towering rage at the decision of the chiefs, and, as he could not have W—— for a slave, he determined no one else should. He tried many times by hints, &c., to get up a feeling against him and have him killed, but always failed, till one day he stated he had dreamt that W—— was endeavouring to take his life. This of course was a matter of high treason; but still the proof was not quite patent, and accuser and owner agreed to have recourse to the mode of divination known as *te hiu* or *toro-toro*. They walked down to a pool of water, W—— accompanying them, and the latter's enemy took two straws. One he named after himself, the other after W——; both he launched into the pool, intently watching the result. In the first instance the straws separated; another trial was attended with the same result; but the third proved decisive, for W—— —*i.e.*, his straw, floated across and under the native's representative. Had it floated over, it would have been a sign that W—— did intend mischief, Pukerangi could not have saved his slave, and W—— would have been most certainly knocked on the head.

CHAPTER II.

MISCELLANEOUS ADVENTURES.

In 1834, in consequence of an old dispute about the Tamaki lands, the Ngatiteata, Ngatitamaho, and Ngatiwhatua, with a few auxiliaries, attacked the Ngatipaoa at Whakatiwai, in hopes of accomplishing the slaughter of Tauwhare, Te Kupenga, and other chiefs. On the invading party's way across from Maramarua, about half way, at a place called the Takanga, they attacked a small party of the Ngatipaoa who were there cultivating. During the attack, a woman of the Ngatipaoa, named Kirikiri, behaved most courageously, loading and firing from a whare in which she was alone by herself, and greatly annoying the Waikatos; she was ultimately dispatched by volleys fired into the whare. By the time the *taua* had reached Whakatiwai, the Ngatipaoa were aware of the intended attack, and contrived to evade it by leaving the pa; but some of the younger members of the *taua* succeeded in capturing several children, who were treated most cruelly by being made fast to legs of *patakas* (a store house built on posts to prevent rats from getting at corn, &c.) as marks for spear practice, and were left to linger during the pleasure of their tormentors. In consequence of the unprovoked attack on the Ngatipaoa, complications arose in Waikato, in which the Ngatinaho and Ngatihine, from their relationship with the Ngatipaoa, endeavoured to obtain redress from the other party. Two engagements were the result, one at Momoreti, in which two of Te Keha's sons were killed; they, with a portion of their force, having left the pa, an engagement (*he parekura*) took place in which the two above named fell; the attacking party escaped scathless. The Ngatinaho party a short time after returned the compliment by attacking the **Ngatitamaho, &c.,** in their pa at Te **Horo,** in which engagement the Ngatinaho lost one of their chiefs, Te Wheoro, killed, and the Ngatitamaho party lost a chief named Tirua, son of Paengahuru; there was also an old woman killed by a shot fired into the pa. An incident showing the devotion of a wife to her husband occurred after this action. On Te Wheoro's being removed from the scene of his death, he was laid out in state, dressed in new mats, his head decorated with feathers. It is customary for a deceased chief to be attended by his wife, or wives as the case may be; in case of a plurality the *rangatira* dame taking precedence as mourner to receive the relatives who come to weep over the *tupapaku*. It was the usual thing to crop the widow's hair as a demonstration of grief, and at the same time as a great disfigurement. In the case of Te Wheoro's widow, a young woman who had a good head of hair, she declined to conform to the rule, and persisted in not having her hair destroyed, remarking that she would make a bad appearance when placed in a position similar to that of her deceased husband. From this remark her relatives guessed her intentions, but, notwithstanding their watching her, she contrived to get her husband's musket, loaded it, tied a piece of flax to the trigger and to her own toe, discharged the piece into her mouth, and scattered her brains far and near.

By the intervention of Te Uira and other influential chiefs, hostilities were suppressed and peace established. On the return of Te Wherowhero with the Ngatiwhatua, the Ngatiteata, the Ngatitamaho, &c., from the march to Manakau, peace was made with the Ngatipaoas, &c., at a large meeting held at Otahuhu for the purpose. In 1834, it being reported that another Ngapuhi expedition was intended against the

Waikato, all the Waikato tribes conjointly erected a large pa at Ngaruawahia, occupying many acres, and it was not till about the election of Potatau as King that the palisading of the pa was entirely demolished.

A misunderstanding arose between the Ngatiteata and the Ngatitamaho tribes respecting the ownership of certain lands in the neighbourhood of Waiuku (Te Whakaupuku) which ultimately resulted in a fight at Taurangaruru. There were also at the same time in the Waikato two tribes, the Ngatipou and the Ngatitipa, disputing about a small difference of boundary amounting only to a few acres, and in the other quarrel the Ngatipous were assisting the Ngatiteata. At the fight at Taurangaruru, near Waiuku, Te Kuri, a chief of the Ngatiteata, and two chiefs of the Ngatipou, Reihana and Moehaka, were killed; a slave of the Ngatitamaho, on the other side, was wounded, and afterwards died.

The row between the Ngatipou and the Ngatitipa brought forward as the grounds of dispute was respecting a strip of about three chains long on the Ihutaroa property containing from about 12 to 15 acres; but there was an old sore in the back ground. They had been sparring for nearly a year by themselves, and nothing serious had resulted till an ally, by an indiscreet movement, involved the two parties in a fight in which three were shot, two of the Ngatipou and one of the Ngatitipa.

A month subsequently another engagement took place, occasioned by one of the Whakauru of the Ngatipou, who was sparring on the boundary with the opposite party, receiving a blow which produced blood. On this, he immediately discharged his piece, wounding one of the opponents, and causing a general engagement, in which 17 were killed and several wounded, some so seriously that their recovery was miraculous. One chief had received three musket wounds, one striking him a little above the knee, running along the bone, and settling in the posterior; one through the leg under the knee joint; and one in the instep, though this latter was not very serious, he being able to extract the ball at the time, as it was a spent one; yet, though no bone was broken, the wound remained open for some time. Notwithstanding these serious wounds I met him the following day on his return from a *taua toto*, at which he had danced the war dance with the rest, and he never laid up on account of them. The Ngatipou and Ngatitcata suffered most severely. The Ngatipou had become dispirited, and sent for me; from the advice I gave them they became reassured, and the action I took with the Ngatitipa was, I believe, the means of staying hostilities, and of the establishment of peace. I had a good understanding with both parties.

In 1832, a quarrel arose among the Ngatipou regarding the ownership of an eel weir on the Whangape Lake. It was at first merely a family feud, and they met to talk the affair over; an altercation ensued, they had brought arms with them, and a piece was discharged wounding in the foot a slave, who, from the pain and irritation of the moment, without hesitation retaliated upon Mauri (the party claiming the eel weir) with a spear he held in his hand. This settled the matter in a very summary manner, each party withdrawing, though swearing vengeance against the other. Mauri died from the spear wound, and nothing more was done in it; his people put up with the loss of their man and of their claim to the eel weir, if they ever had any.

In 1832, a friend who was residing with me had an excellent double-barrelled gun which he prized very much from its having been a present from his relatives on his leaving England. The chief Piraoa having seen the gun requested permission to have it to exhibit to his friends, *tuparas* (two barrels) in those days being a novelty with the Maoris. Piraoa went off to the Thames on a fishing excursion, and some one

E

remarked that he was safe to give away the *tupara*. To save
the gun it was incumbent that Piraoa should be followed,
and I started in company with a Mr. Monteith and six native
lads. We procured a canoe and went up the Awaroa to
Waiuku, crossed over, went along the banks where I had
previously got bogged, but this time more cautiously, without
any great risk to life or limb, and near the Karaka we fell
in with a party of the Ngatiteata fishing, who kindly put us
across to Pukaki, to the astonishment of the natives we met
there, we being the first Europeans who had crossed that sheet
of water. We remained with them that night, and in the
morning proceeded across the country to Otahuhu, fortunately
again getting a lift from there in a canoe to Mangemangeroa,
where we overtook the party we were in search of. By the
time we got there our provisions had become exhausted, and
we had to content ourselves with fern root and sharks' eggs,
or fern root alone. I succeeded in securing the object of our
trip, and, having rested ourselves for a couple of days, the
natives kindly offered to take us in their canoes to Whakatiwai to shorten our road back. We got as far as Taupo
(on the Thames), where they had to land us, the sea being
too heavy after passing the shelter of Waiheke, and we had
to tramp on foot over shingle the remaining distance to
Whakatiwai. From travelling over the shingle we lost
the soles of our shoes, but, notwithstanding, we went on
after dark in expectation of reaching a European's house
which, we were made to understand, was at the very branch
where we were to strike off for the Waikato. We continued on, fatigued and foot sore and in the dark, till at
last we were compelled to give in, and camp out on the
beach in the best way we could. At daylight in the morning, to our surprise and disgust, we found that we had laid
ourselves on the hard shingle without any bedding within
a stone's throw of the very house we had been in search of the

night before. We were not long in rousing out the owner, whose name was Jones, a person trading for Messrs. Jones and Walker, merchants of Sydney, and he received and treated us very kindly for two days, whilst we recruited ourselves and patched up our boots the best way we could. We then proceeded on our journey across to the Mangatawhiri, where we still carried our good fortune, and succeeded in obtaining a canoe and paddles. A twelve hours' row brought us down to Putataka, from whence we had started.

We waited a long time for the return of the vessel to take away the flax, and supply us with stores for trading, as our stock was nearly exhausted with the purchases made. A good look-out to sea was always kept, and at last a vessel hove in sight; but, before she could reach the bar, the wind shifted, and precluded her entering, so she had to drop anchor outside. That was in the forenoon; she did not appear to resemble the "Sydney Packet," and we wondered what vessel she could be. In the afternoon another hove in sight, but this was also a stranger, and the wonderment continued. They remained at anchor 14 days, the wind continuing from the eastward, blowing right out. At last it veered a little, and one vessel, the nearest in to the bar, managed to get just inside, when the wind shifted back to the eastward, preventing the vessel outside from entering; the one that had got in was the "Harlequin." She dropped anchor inside the bar in quiet water, and got up to the anchorage by the next flood tide. From the master we learnt that the "Sydney Packet" had been sold in Sydney, and that the "Samuel," now outside, was sent down to relieve her. I was told that Captain Payne, on hearing of his interest having been sold, agreed to dispose of the flax in my store to the master of the "Harlequin," but I at once made arrangements to secure and retain it for the "Samuel." The next morning seven natives and myself went towards the bar in

a large war canoe, and by the time we had got there the
"Samuel" was under weigh. The natives perceiving this
asked me if I intended going out over the bar. Not imagining that they would go, I said I would leave it to them,
and to my astonishment they said, "Very well, then; we
will go." I didn't half like the idea, for the rollers were
coming in tolerably large. The natives buckled their mats
round them, six went forward, and one, the chief Te Karekare (afterwards Wiremu Paerata), remained aft with me
to steer. We got out very well, excepting that we had
a narrow escape of coming to grief from one roller breaking under us. Fortunately, the natives sitting forward in
the canoe, the sea broke abaft the midships, and as the
preponderance of weight was forward the sea passed under
her; when it broke, the stern was hanging over the gulf
and we were looking down into it. We got on board of
the vessel, and the master, hearing of the trick that was
intended to be played him, determined at all risks to
attempt to work the vessel in over the bar. He con-
sulted the chiefs, Piraoa who was on board with him, and Te
Karekare who had gone out with me, and upon their telling
him they knew the channel, he undertook it. We had made
about three boards (the tide flowing at the time) when
an immense roller came over our broadside, smashing both
bulwarks a-midships, breaking a boat, carrying overboard
a native, and nearly myself. I was immersed up to my
neck and off my feet, and should have gone had not I seized
hold of a ratlin and held fast until the vessel rose and the
water passed off her decks. When she rose she had sufficient
way to go about, and in doing this a bight was made in the
painter of our canoe towed aft; the man overboard managed
to grasp it, and was dragged on board; but the poor fellow
was awfully frightened. He was a fair complexioned
native, and, losing his colour, the blue tatooing on his face

was most beautifully clear, the design and execution being
so good. Captain Payne attempted to carry things with
a high hand, but the master of the "Samuel" was not to be
intimidated, and, after a great deal of bounce on their part,
we shipped the flax on board our vessel and prepared for sea.
I intended to return to Sydney, and arranged accordingly
with the master. The bar being heavy and the wind in
shore, we had to wait a few days for an improvement,
and, during that time, a quarrel arose between a chief,
Te Haupatai (the father of Mohi te Ahi a te Ngu), and his
wife. This was seized upon by Te Pepene Te Tihi, her
brother, as a cause for a row, they being joint owners
of the lands at Pukaki in the Manakau and of a por.
tion of the Tamaki, near Auckland. It was arranged that
they should have a meeting; accordingly Te Haupatai went
out in front of the settlement and sat down with a *taiaha* by
his side to receive Te Tihi, and several of us went with him.
Te Tihi advanced with a *timata* balanced in his hand, while
Te Haupatai, not anticipating an aggressive attack, was
unprepared. The real etiquette which Te Tihi ought to have
followed, if he meant any evil, was this : He should have
advanced, shaking his weapon, then retired ; advanced again,
once more gone back ; and, on his third forward movement,
have then delivered his blow. All this would have been
proper and fair; indeed, so much was love of fair play engrafted
in the disposition of the natives that in many instances the
advancing party, seeing his adversary unarmed, has brought
with him two weapons, and politely handed one of them to
the *tupapaku* (lit., corpse), as the other man is called; thus
honourably placing his opponent on even terms with himself.
In this case, however, Te Tihi struck him on his first advance.
Te Haupatai, though wounded, rose and struggled with Te
Pepene, and Te Haupatai's party, seeing that he was hit,
called for muskets ; Te Pepene retired, and a musketry action

commenced. At the time Te Haupatai was struck I was standing at his back, and hearing the call for arms another European and myself ascended a hill and looked down on the engagement which lasted for about half an hour without any serious results, no one being hit. Hostilities were suspended temporarily, each party having a war dance as if intending to renew it. Te Haupatai died two days after my departure, but the whole thing ultimately ended in smoke; for, two years after, the family of Te Haupatai were living amicably with their uncle Te Pepene in the same settlement, and appeared to be on the best of terms. Two days after, I left for Sydney, and, after remaining there about a month, took my passage for New Zealand via Van Diemen's Land in the same vessel. It was now the equinox, and we made a dreadful passage of 16 days, having to put in to Jervis Bay and another place, near Twofold Bay, from stress of weather. We carried away fore-topmast, gaff, spanker boom, and had a boat washed away from her davits; and, to me the most grievous sight, the goats, poultry, &c., I had on board and intended for use in New Zealand one by one disappeared away to leeward. Whilst in Twofold Bay we availed ourselves of the opportunity of getting fresh water and firewood; but, while getting them, a party of blacks put in an appearance. Two men, more bold than the rest, advanced towards us, and a couple of natives that were returning to New Zealand being ashore with us, I got them to give a Maori yell to try its effect on the New Hollanders. It so frightened them that they jumped up at once and bolted off, and I verily believe, if they have not died or stopped from fatigue, they must be running still.

A curious error on the captain's part occurred on this trip. We got into a dense fog when, by the captain's reckoning, two hundred miles out at sea; there was, however, a curious appearance ahead which a native declared was Mount Egmont, at Taranaki, but the skipper being appealed to pooh-poohed the idea. It was, however, lucky for us that a breeze springing up dissipated the fog, as this was the mountain and we were close to the breakers. We were fortunate in having a smart craft under us, else it might have gone hard with vessel and crew. We reached Waikato Heads in safety, but, the captain knowing nothing of the channel and entrusting the pilotage to the natives on board, we managed to get ashore, and this time for good. The Maoris behaved very well, helping to unload cargo, dismantle the vessel, &c., and not a single article was lost. The crew got very drunk, some of them being hauled on shore through the surf to save their lives, and eventually the vessel went to pieces. A short time after the wreck a misunderstanding arose between the captain and myself respecting the ownership of a cannon which I had purchased in Sydney and shipped as my property. The captain had only joined the vessel on the eve of her departure, and, being perhaps unaware of my rights to the piece, he wanted to sell it to raise money to pay himself and crew. Of course I was as anxious to retain my own property, and the consequence was that, on my refusing to give it up, he sent up a posse of 14 hands, as the gun, being a 12-pounder and heavy, required some strength to move it. The proceedings began by their reeving a rope through a ring at the breech to haul it down, but, though single-handed to contend with the party, I was not going to give in, even though my pakeha servant would not help me. In those days I was young and strong, and when the captain and his son attempted to hustle me, I tripped up the son, caught the father by the collar and breech and pitched him on to the son. Whilst this was going on, the party were dragging the gun away, though slowly; but the rope they had fastened had taughtened nicely and so invitingly that I could not resist the temptation, and, with one slash of my knife, I cut it asunder,

sending the haulers tumbling over one another to the great
amusement of the Maori lookers-on. Being laughed at did
not improve my friends' tempers, and they seemed determined
to take the gun, but I too had become warm, and was equally
resolved they should not have it; so, when again they made
the rope fast to the gun, I took up a pair of pistols I had
fetched from the house and declared that if they persisted I
would shoot the man nearest to the gun. This mild threat
had the effect of inducing each of them to avoid proximity,
and there was a general falling back, although the captain
urged them to continue. On seeing the determined air I had
assumed, and fearing something serious might happen, Te
Karekare jumped up and declared that he would not permit
so many to attack a single individual, and that, if they went
on, he would assist me. This decided the question, the
pakehas retired grumbling, and I was left in peaceable
possession of the gun.

After this, I commenced trading in flax, and Reihana
called one day and requested to see my trade. He selected
a musket, though he did not take it away, but merely marked
it by attaching a piece of string, at the same time telling me
he would only give one basket of flax for it, the customary
price being 27 or 28 baskets containing 7 cwt. A few days
after, on looking up the river (our house faced the water), I
perceived an extremely singular-looking body looming in the
distance and coming down stream. On its approaching
nearer it looked, through the glass, like a haystack built on
canoes; we could see the paddles glisten in the sun as they
were worked to propel the body towering above them. On
their nearing us, it turned out to be Reihana with about 40
companions and the single basket of flax that he had stated
he would give for the musket. Two canoes had been fastened
together a short distance apart, on which was erected a stage,
and on this was placed the "basket." When the tide had

receded and the canoes were left dry, it took all the forty
natives to lift and carry it into the store. Reihana objected
to having it weighed, stating that if it was less than the usual
quantity I must put up with the loss, and, if it was more, he
was satisfied, as it was his proposition not to have it weighed ;
he then took his musket and returned with the flood tide.
Afterwards, on pressing my flax for shipment, I had the
curiosity to weigh this monster basket, and found that it was
over 8 cwt. instead of 7 cwt., the usual price.

In the autumn of 1832, I took a trip up the country to
trade, and during my absence a report reached us that the
Ngapuhis had arrived at Port Waikato. The natives in the
vicinity of the settlement at which I was stopping, mustered
about 300 in number, and with them I went in company to
my home. On my arrival I found the Maoris had mustered
from all directions, and, moreover, that some had been
troublesome to the man-servant I had left in charge ; but
Reihana, on his arrival with his party, hearing of the annoy-
ance my servant had experienced, told him that if his men
were permited to establish themselves in the fore-court it would
probably check the importunity and pilfering of the others,
a propensity for which they had exhibited some inclination.
After he had taken charge nothing further occurred, though
there were 3,000 natives, as stated in page 19, surrounding us.

The abduction of Mr. W—— has been stated at page 20.
He afterwards returned to Waikato and resided at Kopokowhatitiri, at which place a large pa, or, more properly speaking, three pas joined together, had been erected, as three
tribes were living in it, each party having built the portion
in which they resided. One chief having taken liberties with
the wife of a chief of another tribe, a quarrel arose and
threatened to become serious ; but, through the intervention
of several chiefs, an amicable arrangement was made, which
so elated the highest in rank that he determined to give the

F

assembled people a feast.   On inquiry, he discovered that he
had no *kinaki* (relish) handy to give with the potatoes and
kumeras, and so he was rather at a loss; but, on consideration, he bethought himself what a treat a nice tender young
woman would be.   By-and-by one of his numerous wives
came out, and proved the use wives can be put to on an
emergency.   She was directed to fetch firewood and prepare a *hangi* (a *hangi* is the native oven, in which food is
cooked, or, more properly, steamed); unconscious for what
purpose this was intended, she went on with the work imagining that it was for the usual routine of cooking; but, on its
completion, she was seized, and it then flashed across her mind
that she was the proposed victim.   In her fear and agony she
called to her husband and chief for protection, but the brute's
only response was "Karanga mai! karanga mai!" (call to me;
call to me), and a laugh.   She was killed and cooked, and the
party ate, drank, made peace, and were merry while picking
her bones.   While I am on the theme of murder, I may
mention another case of woman slaughter which occurred at
Whaingaroa.   On my paying Mr. Lonsdale a visit in 1833,
and while stopping at his house, I was one morning informed
by a chief that the natives living on the opposite side of the
river, at Orea, had killed a woman and apparently meant to
eat her, as she was at that time being cooked.   I informed
Mr. Lonsdale, the master of a vessel that was in harbour,
and two other Europeans, and we determined to go across
and deprive them of their anticipated repast by disturbing
the *hangi* in which we expected she would be stewing.   We
crossed the river and, on nearing the shore, saw a number
of children amusing themselves with something which seemed
to afford them great delight.   On landing we discovered that
the head of the unfortunate woman was the plaything which
they were rolling about; they were laughing and jumping
all the time like a number of little imps.   Mr. Lonsdale at

once picked it up and, wrapping it in his handkerchief, placed it in the boat. We then proceeded inland to carry out the object of our visit; but, to our surprise and disgust, the natives had anticipated the object of our visit and had formed themselves round the *hangi* in a circle, which we were not permitted to enter. We remained there a considerable time thinking that perhaps they might relax in their vigilance; but no, they did sentry-go, relieving each other till our patience was exhausted and we retired. We returned home, and in the evening Mr. Lonsdale and the captain re-visited them to see the "wild beasts" feed. In this they were successful, and were invited to join in and partake of the savory meal; but they very politely declined, the captain merely requesting the little finger of the unfortunate woman, which he obtained and preserved as a souvenir. On my first seeing the head bowled about by the children, as we landed from the boat, I thought I recognized the features, but could not call to memory where I had seen them, the jaw having fallen and the dirt about the face having altered the appearance; but I learnt afterwards that she was a slave belonging to the tribe under whose protection I was living in Waikato. She had run away to the chief who afterwards killed her, by whom she was taken as a supernumerary wife; but, finding her inconstant, he had knocked her on the head and disposed of her as stated above.

The only murder of a European committed in the Waikato District previous to the war in '63 was by one white man on another. Two men, Charlie —— and Geordy Clare, lived together at Whaingaroa, when, one day, apparently without provocation (as was stated by the natives), no other Europeans being near, Clare shot Charlie with a pistol in the side, and ultimately dispatched him by jumping on him and otherwise brutally ill-treating him. There being no law in New Zealand at the time, he committed the act with impunity, though afterwards, having confessed the murder, he was taken to Sydney by Captain Kent in the "Lord Byron" brig. On their reaching Sydney he was handed over to the authorities, and the charge of murder preferred against him upon his own confession. On his examination, being asked by the Court what he had to say to the charge, he stated that it was certainly true he had said that he had murdered the man, but that he had made the statement as a ruse to obtain a passage out of New Zealand, as he had no money or property to meet the expense. From the want of evidence, he was liberated, but he was shortly afterwards drowned on his first trip to sea; the vessel foundered, and all hands were lost, not one appearing to tell the tale, and Clare no doubt being the "Jonah."

CHAPTER III.

A Hodge-Podge of Reminiscences.

On my leaving Waikato at the time of the anticipated attack by the Ngapuhis, I went to reside at Te Horo, a settlement on the Waipa, where I was living when the Waikatos mustered to follow the Ngapuhis. During their absence I determined to shift my quarters, and made arrangements with other natives to bring canoes and take my property. I had nearly cleared the house of the moveables, and sent the canoes away loaded, when I got a hint from a pakeha living near me that it was intended to rob me. Very soon after, I perceived a posse of about a dozen natives approach the gate ; three entered and the rest remained outside. On the three entering the house, after the usual salutations, I asked them their object. I should mention that as soon as I got the hint that they were coming, I provided myself with a musket, buckled a cartridge box on, placed cartridges between the fingers of my left hand after the most approved native style, and suspended a dirk stick from my wrist. This latter article was the terror of the natives. It had been a sword stick and got broken, upon which I shortened it sufficiently to permit its being carried in the trousers' pocket; it was one of those that had the dirk thrown from the end. Seeing me so well prepared for them, they became confused and said that, having heard that I was about leaving their settlement, they had come to see me before I went away. I told them that I was well aware of their intention, and suggested they should weigh the matter well before

acting, for the first person who attempted to take anything
or to molest me I would not hesitate to shoot; and that,
before they could dispatch me, I would have two or three
more of them.   They went on excusing themselves by saying
that they had merely come to see me before my departing
and leaving the house, but on their way out I heard them say
to those who had remained outside that it wouldn't do, as I
was prepared for them.   They had not left me long when
I received another message informing me that they were
going in pursuit of my canoes to strip them, and I immediately
started by land to join the party in charge, a European.
Passing the end of the pa in which the natives resided, I
found them launching a canoe; but on seeing me they
desisted, and asked me where I was going.   I told them
I was going to shoot ducks: " Ah, ah," they said, " you
think to shoot ducks that can't fly !"   I went on, overtook my canoes, and informed my servant of the intended
muru, or robbery; telling him in Maori to shoot the first
man who touched anything in the canoe, then to throw his
musket into the water and defend himself with his cutlass.
A native lad who had followed me heard my instructions,
and rushed back to his people, who, of course, as I had
expected, had broken into and robbed my house.   It was not,
however, the party I had seen; they had, on my passing
them, desisted from launching their canoe, and gone up to
the house; but, on seeing how little property there was and
how useless, the principal of the party remarked it would be
folly to interfere with anything there, for on my return, if
I found the things gone, I would set fire to my house, and,
from its close proximity to those in the pa, the whole settlement would be burned; so they left without touching anything.   But another party, thinking they might have a finger
in the pie, walked off with two or three trifles, amongst
which were an iron pot, some provision I had retained for

my support during the absence of the canoes, and a dog.
I soon learnt who had perpetrated the theft, and went immediately in search of the delinquent. On entering that
part of the pa where he lived, I saw my dog tied up to the
fence and the man who had taken it sneaking away. I
followed in pursuit, but by the time I had got out he had
disappeared, having run down a slope in front of the pa and
hidden in the high fern. I followed on his track, and came
upon him; thinking he had the iron pot with him, I declared
if he did not give it me I would shoot him, at the same time
cocking my musket. This so intimidated him that he jumped
up, throwing open his mat to show he had not got it. I felt
sure he had hidden it, and foolishly looked for it, turning my
back towards him, which he availed himself of by clasping
me round the waist from behind, at the same time endeavouring to throw me; in this he, fortunately, did not succeed,
though he was doing his best, and uttering all kinds of
threats. I took it very coolly; and fearing that in the
struggle the piece, being loaded and cocked, might go off and
perhaps wound some of the spectators, I requested a lad to
take it. As soon as the gun was out of my hands, my friend,
imagining I was unarmed, became outrageous; fortunately
I had my pocket companion, the dirk-stick, with me, and,
unperceived by him, I got it out and gave him a prod or two,
the last one having the effect of making him loose his hold
and bolt off at a great rate. I had a little difficulty in
regaining my gun as it had been stolen from where the lad
had hidden it; the sister of the chief under whose protection
I had been living took the matter up, threatening the delinquent with any amount of *makutu* (witchcraft) if it was not
produced immediately. The same evening I had it returned
to me, and on my leaving I presented it to her as an acknowledgment of her kindness.

The only case of quarrel in which I struck a native

occurred at this settlement, and that was in self-defence. A man named Te Kakare, who had been in the habit of frequenting my house, used, without my permission, a knife I kept for killing pigs; during his absence **I wanted** the **knife,** but, not finding it, I had to let the pig go, and put out the fire. On his return from work he brought it back, and I remonstrated with him for not asking permission before taking it, at the same time telling him to leave the premises and never presume to come there again. To my surprise he rushed at me with his head down, meaning to clasp me round the legs and throw me; but I fancy he was a little astonished when I jerked up my knee into his face, bringing him upright, and followed this up with my fists right and left. Down he went, the blood rushing copiously from his nose; he was not yet satisfied, for up he got, rushed at me again, and I had to repeat the dose. This might have gone on, but a chief, who happened to be sitting in the house at the time, seeing what was up, called out to him to know if he wished to be killed, and told him to clear out, which he did. The next morning on my rising, a little after daylight, I found six large baskets of potatoes and a fine hog tied to the fence near the gate, and was told they were Te Kakare's. I thought they were brought for sale, and so, from his conduct the day before, I refused to purchase them; but I was undeceived, and told they were there as *utu* or reparation for his conduct of the day before; I declined to accept them, but the fine was enforced by the chief. Te Kakare did not put in an appearance for a length of time, but at last he came to me and we made friends; I paid him secretly for his goods, and we have remained on capital terms ever since.

On my going to Toroakapakapa, the natives built me a house, and I settled down quietly waiting for advices from Sydney, which, by the way, I never received. I had been there some time when two gentlemen from the Thames paid me a visit, and I accompanied them on their return after their remaining with me a fortnight. On the way we had to cross the Waikato, and, in the absence of a canoe, we managed it on a *moki*. A *moki* is a quantity of flag or bulrush tied together, and from its buoyancy when dry will support a considerable weight. We then ascended the Maungakawa range, and descended into the Kawheriki Valley, in which we came across a corpse suspended by the heels from a tree, and, a little further on, a head. In the bottom of the valley was a deserted pa that had been set on fire, probably by accident, as we saw amongst the remains portions of burnt guns and a few iron pots, both articles, in those days, very scarce and consequently valuable; by some accident the pa may have become *tapued*, and its inhabitants fired it to get rid of the *tapu*. It appears that, during the quarrel between the Ngatihaua and the Ngatipaoa, &c., the latter, with a party of Ngapuhi, made a raid upon the Ngatihaua at Kawheriki; Ngatihaua sallied out, attacked the assailants, and succeeded in capturing three of the Ngapuhi, one of whom they suspended alive by the heels, the other two they killed, decapitating them, placing the heads on stumps of trees, and eating their bodies: the other head we saw in the vicinity of the pa at Matamata. The treatment the captured men received so intimidated the rest of their party that they were off before the next morning. On the Matamata plains the remains of two pas, within a few chains of each other, were pointed out to me as the spot where the occupants kept on fighting for three days and, like the Cockney sportsman who was out all day and shot nothing, had committed no execution, but withdrew by mutual consent.

In 1834, being short of necessary stores, I made a second trip to Kopu, on the Thames, accompanied by a European; this time we crossed the Frith of the Thames from Whaka-

tiwai. We remained a week and obtained what we went
for; but, leaving the Waiho, or Thames proper, we found
the sea too heavy to cross; consequently our chief, Te Aho,
recommended our going into Kauaeranga (the present Short-
land), and remaining until the wind and sea dropped. We
were met in a very friendly way by the natives, chiefly out
of courtesy to the chief who accompanied us. In the morning we took a walk about the settlement, and seeing a nice
little piece of secluded bush without any *powrheros* (a *pou-
whero* is a post painted red, and indicating a *tapued* spot) to
intimidate us, curiosity induced me to inspect it, and I did
so without remark, probably from my not having been seen;
but my companion, when going over the same place under
the impression that a similar excursion would do him good,
was seen coming out of it, and a most serious rumpus occurred,
as, unfortunately, this was stated to be a most sacred burial-
place. The first intimation I had of the affair was from
seeing several natives rushing to seize their muskets to shoot
the individual who had presumed to desecrate their *tapu whaka-
harahara* (an important *tapu*). I caught hold of the object of
their displeasure, covered his body with mine, and hustled him
into the whare where our chief Te Aho was quietly sleeping
unconscious of anything wrong. We were pretty sharp in
waking him up, and when he heard the particulars of the
grievous insult offered to his pakehas, he sprang out of the
house into the open space in front and demanded to know
who had presumed to affront him in such a way as to even
talk about molesting his pakeha? He considered he had
shown great condescension in permitting his pakehas to visit
them, not quite recollecting at the time that he was making
a virtue of necessity, as we had been driven in there by
stress of weather, and were making a convenience of them.
Anyhow, as it was always customary to entertain visitors,
and that usually with the best the *tangata whenua* (land folk)

had, he insisted upon their launching our craft (a large war canoe) immediately, that we might depart from such inhospitable shores, and we did so, notwithstanding the boisterousness of the weather. We had a large native sail made of raupo or bullrush, and went scudding away, but for a while it was so rough that we did not dare to make a straight course, and we edged along the land till we got to the opposite side of the Frith where we had to haul our wind to pass round a point at Pukorokoro. This was done all right, but at the next point we had to strike the sail, and, finding that no headway could be made against the sea, the canoe was beached half-filled with water, and all our clothing, of course, saturated; notwithstanding this, however, and to add to our distress, some of the Ngatipaoa made a *taua* on one of our party for a real or imaginary offence, took some few articles from the natives, and attempted the same with us Europeans. The natives gave up their property with a good grace, but we declined to surrender what we had gone so far to procure and had overcome so many difficulties to obtain. Te Aho, having lost some trifles, was not to be done. The wily old boy set to work and ransacked his memory as to former doings. A happy thought struck him, and he was delighted at being able to recollect that, at some time or other, the Ngatipaoa had committed a breach of etiquette with regard to his tribe. He forthwith made a *taua* upon them, and in it obtained a considerable amount of property, not at all a bad return for the few things that his people had lost.

This visit to the Thames reminds me of a story told formerly of a captain of a trader, who used to visit Tauranga. He was there with his vessel in 1831 or 1832, and, having taken a dislike to a certain chief (who had made himself, certainly, obnoxious to the Europeans generally), endeavoured to poison him with oxalic acid; failing in this, he deliberately shot him as he was leaving the vessel's side in his

canoe, the vessel at the time being under weigh and leaving
the port. The murdered native's companions pulled ashore
in the canoe with the dead body, and, to their joy, saw that
the wind had dropped, and that the vessel was floating help-
lessly about between Te Papa and Maunganui. Revenge
seemed at hand; they were strong in numbers, the Europeans but few; the very winds were on their side; and, with
loud shouts, they hastily manned a number of large canoes.
Meanwhile all on board thought themselves lost; and, if
there be such a thing as conscience about a South Sea trader,
the skipper must have felt uncomfortable; luckily for them
a puff of wind came just in time to take them outside. The
natives, however, were not going to be done out of *utu*, so
they got up a party to attack a man who was trading for the
skipper to the southward. As usual, the object of the expedition got wind, and the individual for whose benefit it was
intended was on his guard. There was another European,
also a trader, living in the neighbourhood, and he agreed to
make common cause with the captain's man. The bales of
flax were moved into one house and disposed along the sides
so as to afford protection (they were ball-proof against the
muskets then in use); all the arms, ammunition, &c., which
they could lay hands on were got together, and the two men
prepared for a regular siege. On came the *taua* and, surrounding the place, demanded a surrender; the answer was,
of course, a shot, and the departure of one of the assailants to
his "happy hunting grounds;" and this was the signal for a
general assault. It was a case of life or death for the two
pakehas, and they did their best, the one loading while the
other fired. A good many natives were knocked over, but
an unlucky shot came in, killing one of the two. The natives
outside soon discovered there was something wrong and made
a rush, which succeeded; they reserved the survivor for
future death and "kai," plundered all the trade, and burned

the house with the dead man in it. It was very comfortably arranged that the prisoner should be put to death in the evening as a sweet morsel of revenge for the chief shot at Tauranga ; but in the interval another chance of additional vengeance seemed at hand ; there was actually a vessel in the offing, evidently intending to speak the shore. Here was a prospect of utilising the pakeha and obtaining *utu* by a good wholesale slaughter, not to mention a decent chance of loot. The prisoner was told, on pain of instant death, to signal the vessel. He did so, and a whaleboat approached the shore ; he was ordered to entice the boat close in, and this was the ticklish moment ; luckily none of the Maoris understood English, so, putting on an air of nonchalance, the poor wretch called out to his countrymen, whatever they did, not to row in stem first, but to back in. He told them he was a prisoner, and that he was going to make a bold stroke for liberty. The crew did as they were bid, each man nerving himself up to the task ; and, while the boat was in the midst of the breakers, and the natives were licking their lips in anticipation of their horrible feast, the prisoner dashed into the water, seized the gunwale, and held on tight while the rowers bent their backs and gave way with a will. So astounded was each Maori that the whole lot got out of range, and the rescued man was hauled in before a shot was fired.*

While on the theme of murder, I may mention an episode that occurred between two individuals personally known to myself. Manukawehi, a slave belonging to a chief of one of the tribes of Waikato, ran away with his wife to the Ngatipaoa in the Thames ; but, having discovered some impropriety in the conduct of his wife, and having no lawyer to advocate his cause or Divorce Court to appeal to, he thought

---

* NOTE.—It is not long ago that I heard an old Maori chief relate the latter part of this story identically with the above particulars. —J. St. J.

he would simplify the matter by making away with her; he
dug a hole in the ground, cajoled her in the dark to the edge,
tripped her up into it, and buried her, as he hoped, alive.
Thinking that he had finally disposed of her, he went back
home, chuckling quietly, and keeping his act a secret. During
the night the wife, only stunned by the blow, contrived to
get out of the hole, went up to the house where her husband
was sleeping, sat at the door, and added fuel to the fire,
which had nearly burnt out. On its blazing up, the man
awoke, and, perceiving his wife sitting at the door covered
with earth, just as she had risen from the grave, took her for
a ghost. Frightened was no name for him : down he went,
squatting and groaning, with his head well covered up in his
mat. The wife seemed to enjoy his bother; and after resting
a short time she got up, left the settlement clandestinely, and
reached Auckland. The man kept his own counsel; the
woman remained in Auckland unseen by her husband and
that section of natives residing in his vicinity; and it was
generally believed that she had run away, until one day the
husband confessed to having killed her. She was subsequently seen in Auckland, and was looked upon as a spirit
until she explained how she had managed to escape. It was
not an unusual thing for husbands to kill their wives for in-
continence, or to inflict other modes of punishment as their
fancies might lead them. I have known several instances
of chiefs killing their wives for infidelity.

Derangement of intellect is very prevalent amongst the
Maoris; some are harmless, others mischievous. The majority
have a great liking for fire : I have on several occasions seen
both mad men and mad women with a piece of bark slung
round their necks and suspended in front, as piemen carry
their pies; on the bark they place a little earth and on that
they have their miniature fire which, in the distance, when
smoking, makes them somewhat resemble an itinerant tinker

with his furnace. One case is on record of a man who was daft from his infancy, and who had never left off sucking his mother. When he grew up he left his people and lived in the bush upon what it produced; but at times he would go into the settlement, seek his mother, obtain his accustomed milk, and retire to the bush again. On one occasion she had a very narrow escape from his violence; during one absence, which had lasted longer than usual, her milk had dried up, and the son, imagining that his mother was withholding his nourishment purposely, would have committed some outrage had he not been restrained by the seasonable arrival of some friends, when he decamped off to the bush again.

CHAPTER IV

IT was in 1834 that the Missionaries paid their first visit to Waikato, and a very narrow escape they had. One of the Wesleyan body, with several Ngapuhi natives, after surmounting many difficulties and passing through uninhabited localities, at last reached Waikato. A portion of our party had gone down the river in a canoe when they fell in with the pakeha and his suite, all seated on a *moki* made of raupo, and propelled by poles instead of paddles. The Ngatipo were going in the opposite direction, and their first impulse on hearing the voices and recognising the Ngapuhi dialect was to blaze into them, supposing them to be enemies and the advance guard of a war-party. Fortunately for them, their pakeha made himself conspicuous, which induced a parley, and the object of the visit was then explained; they were brought to the camp, supplied with provisions and a canoe, and sent forward rejoicing the following morning. After their tour through the Waikato they returned to Hokianga, and the pakehas in the north, finding the Waikatos so friendly, started another expedition under the auspices of the Church Missionary Society, and established themselves at Mangapouri (near Alexandra), at the junction of the Puniu and the Waipa. A dispute arose between the two missions as to the right of the field for their operations, the Wesleyans claiming it by priority; and Mr. Hamlin and the Church people withdrew and settled at Mocatoa, in the Manakau. Ultimately a compromise was made, and Mr.

Morgan returned and formed a station at Otawhao where he remained till the war commenced in Waikato, when the clergymen of both denominations had to leave.

Prior to the arrival of the Church missionaries at Mangapouri the natives paid but little heed to the Sunday, though I had a big flagstaff from which used to fly, each Sunday, a flag, and though I had, in a great measure, induced them to stop agricultural pursuits on that day. To obviate this, the Missionaries enlisted my aid to persuade them to build a church, and we succeeded without much trouble.

On the Mission supplying me with books and slates, I undertook the instruction of the natives, and found, to my surprise and gratification, they exhibited a great desire to learn, and the facility with which some advanced was astonishing. I continued to instruct them until I left for Sydney, when I remained away nearly four years, but I occasionally corresponded with them and they with me. In one of Te Uira's letters he requested that I would select and forward down a Missionary as they wished to have one of their own, independent of the other tribes. When the Missionaries had established themselves at Mangapouri, they wished their wives to join them, but a difficulty arose—the absence of chimneys to their dwellings; there was no stone in the vicinity available, the transport of bricks was next to impossible, and without chimneys the houses would be untenable by the ladies. Not having entirely lost my gallantry I was induced, out of sympathy to the ladies and children, to undertake the superintendence of a manufactory of a sufficient number of bricks for the fire-places of two houses. The result far surpassed my expectations, and it was only the other day, after a lapse of 38 years, that I saw pieces which had been left on the ground after the chimneys had been pulled down, and even then they were quite sound, and almost as hard as stone. The manufacture of those bricks verified the saying, that "A man does not know what he can do till he tries."

Accidents from the heedless way in which gunpowder was landed and stored were of common occurrence. The indiscriminate use of the pipe, even while men were employed in serving out powder, on the opening of a cask, or in manufacturing cartridges, &c., led to a good many. On one occasion the Ngatitamaho, anticipating an attack from the Ngapuhis, had opened a cask of gunpowder to distribute amongst the people of the tribe; it was placed in an open area in front of the dwelling-houses, the recipients had arranged themselves in a circle round it, and the dispensers were at work. About two-thirds of the quantity had been disposed of when Te Rangiratahu, a lad of about 13 or 14 years of age, a son of the chief of the tribe, walked up smoking a short pipe with a lighted coal in it, and leaned over to look into the cask; the coal naturally fell from his pipe, and there was a very pretty blow up. Cask staves and fire were sent in all directions; Hika, one of the senior chiefs, was killed; Te Rangiratahu, and several others who formed the circle, were severely burnt; and altogether there was a jolly row. I was sent for to attend Te Rangiratahu, and found the front part of his body burnt from the waist to the crown of the head: at the time of the accident he had but a native mat wrapped round his loins, so that all the upper body was exposed. I took him in hand, and, to exemplify the healthy state of the natives and the quickness with which their sores heal, it is a fact that, by means of simple remedies, I had him convalescent and without a scar in three weeks. Another case was where three young men were making cartridges, and, as usual, could not do without the pipe; by some mishap the powder exploded, and seriously burnt the three. Parauri, the most seriously injured, they brought to me; one they took to the mission station; and the third they

retained and doctored themselves. Parauri was burnt all
over chest, face, and arms ; and when he arrived the parts
scorched were covered with scraped *mamaku* (the edible fern
tree) : the accident had happened about three days previously.
On his arrival, I advised the removal of the *mamaku*; but I had
to contend against a powerful *tohunga* (priest), who advocated
its use. At last I carried my point, with this exception, that
I allowed one arm, that least burnt, to retain the *mamaku*.
He was so much injured about the face that he could not see.
I merely stuck to cleanliness and simple remedies, and on my
return to apply a second dressing, I was informed that my
patient had had no sleep the whole night through pain ; it
was nothing but, " Au—e, au—e !" all night long ; and to my
gratification I was told it arose from the *mamaku*-arm, but
that the parts I had dressed were perfectly free from pain.
I was begged to remove the *mamaku*, which I did with great
reluctance, as the **stench** emanating from it was almost
intolerable, and I am happy to be able to say that in less than
a month he was cured and without a scar. The individual
retained by the natives died ; and the one taken to the
Mission station **recovered** with a stiff arm, useless to him.
A third case was where an old man attempted to commit
suicide. Nikorima Kiwani, a slave, but a favourite with his
chief and people, returning to the settlement after a short
absence, met a chief's wife who had been confined while he
was away : seeing her with something protruding from under
her mat, and at a distance mistaking it for a pumpkin, he
called out to her, " *Maku to paukina* " (give me your pumpkin); but to his horror discovered that he had mistaken the
bald head of a new-born babe for a vegetable. The mother
was very much enraged that her child's head, that very sacred
portion of a very sacred person, should be compared to food,
and that of **so** inferior a description ; so, on discovering
the egregious error he had committed, and in fear of what

the father might do to him, Nikorima deliberately took a fire-
stick into a house which contained a cask of Maori-made
gunpowder, of about 20 lbs., and unceremoniously put the
lighted stick into it. The whare was sent in every direction,
and poor Kiwani (as described by an eye-witness, who
happened to be nearer at the time than he liked) was seen
flying through the smoke, and alighted at a considerable
distance from where he started; notwithstanding his aerial
flight, he recovered with only the loss of the use of one of his
hands. When the parent of little "pumpkin head" heard
of the accident to Kiwani he merely laughed at the mistake
about the child's head.

Even in these early days there used to be some amount
of double-dealing in land transactions. A pakeha would be
anxious to obtain a block of land; he would see the numerous
owners, pay down his money, and fancy himself a landed
proprietor. Presently another lot of natives would put in
a claim, and reference to the sellers in the first instance
would elicit the fact that these latter had a right in the land.
Satisfying these only brought up more, so, what with one
thing and the other, the purchase money was often treble the
value of the land. I have known the same block sold twice
over to the same individual by the Maori owners giving, in
each case, different names to the boundaries, &c. This was
easily done, as most spots have two, if not more, names. In
other cases, lands represented as fertile have proved, on
inspection after the completion of the purchase, to be mere
swamps; and it was impossible to get the deposit money
back.

I was present at the first meeting of the Native Land
League in Waikato. I was then travelling up the Waikato
in a canoe in company with a European lady who was going
to join her husband at Otawhao, and we stopped at Waitutu,
a settlement on the bank of the Waikato river, a little above

Rangiriri, to prepare our mid-day meal. While it was getting ready, I took a stroll and seeing a whare open and a number of natives inside, I popped my head in at the door, was recognised by the inmates, and requested to join them and hear what they were talking about. I remarked that I did **not consider that** I could be interested in what they had met for, but I was told that it concerned both races, pakeha and Maori, and that they were there to arrange a boundary line between the pakeha and Maori lands. The person who was speaking when I interrupted them, was requested to re-commence that I might hear all that had been said, which he did, to the purport that they were jealous of the encroachments of the pakeha ; that, if they got mixed up in the occupation of lands with the Maoris, altercations and unpleasantnesses would arise from the trespass of stock on each other's lands, &c. Then, appealing to me, they said, " You know that we are not able to compete with the pakeha in industry and labour; there are many parts of the country eligible for native cultivation where no timber is growing for fencing, therefore we could not fence, and our crops would be destroyed by our pakeha neighbour's cattle. To prevent that, we have come to the determination of not selling a single acre within a prescribed boundary. On the Auckland side we will not oppose the sale of an acre ; the natives may sell and you may purchase all within that boundary, which we intend shall be the Mangatawhiri Creek to the Waikato Heads one way, and over to Whakatiwai on the Thames the other way." One chief, named Tarapuhi, was rather boisterous, but I very quickly quieted him by telling him that he should be the last to exclaim, as he had clandestinely attempted to sell land to which he had not an iota of claim, and for which he had received a portion of the money (I had happened to have heard of this only a few days previously). He attempted to defend himself ; but, on the rest learning the particulars, he was censured, and he shut up for the remainder of that meeting. The particular reason they assigned for striking a boundary was to separate themselves and their cultivations from the Europeans in dread of complications which might lead to serious results between the two races.

In 1862, a short time previous to the war, Wiremu Tamihana* convened at Peria, in the Upper Waikato, a meeting of all the tribes in the Island to take into consideration the course to be adopted with regard to their King, whom they were determined to support in opposition to the Government. Anticipating a collision with the pakeha, and foreseeing the result of such a war, the unsettled and harrassing life they would lead, he had collected and had cooked as food for the meeting all the indigenous roots and berries that their ancestors had formerly lived upon, to show them that they would probably have to fall back upon the natural products of their country. Many subjects were brought forward for discussion, but one speech above the rest did Wiremu Tamihana great credit. A question was asked, "What should be done with respect to debts due to pakehas;" and this was given to the different *runangas* for consideration; the majority gave it as their opinion that they should not be paid, and some that they should. It was then given to Wiremu Tamihana for his opinion. He scrutinized the numbers on each side, and then spoke very much in these words: "I see the majority are for not paying; but if any of us have incurred a just debt we are in duty bound to settle it; don't let us fall back, as the pakehas do, upon a law (the Statute of Limitations) to free ourselves from our debts; if any of us have incurred a just debt, let it have been incurred when it will, we are in duty bound to pay it. If it should occur that we have a rupture with the pakeha, let us go into the war with clean hands."

---

* The well-known chief William Thompson.

I have had several opportunities of seeing Matutaera, Potatau II., in state. On one occasion I was on business at Horahora, a settlement a short distance below Rangiriri, when it was reported that Matutaera was coming down to see the people of the settlement on state affairs. It was not long after that a messenger arrived informing the *tangata whenuas* (resident natives) that his Majesty was approaching; whereupon everyone turned out to receive him, myself amongst them, as I had stayed out of curiosity to see him. The first indication of the approach of the party was a long streaming flag floating high up in the air, advancing steadily along the margin of the river, his Majesty and suite having come down the river in canoes and, having landed a short distance above the settlement in order to make a display and an impressive entry into the *kainga,* they were soon seen to emerge from amongst the *harakeke* and *toetoe,* a native in advance, carrying the flag. At a short distance behind him came the trumpeter with a *tetero,* or trumpet, made of the leaves of *harakeke,* or green flax; then the advance guard, of thirty men, three abreast, all armed, with one officer—a captain; as a substitute for a band, the body-guard sang Maori songs to English tunes. Next followed his Majesty; after him, his personal friends; and then, his civil attendants; the procession being closed by thirty more armed men and an officer—a subaltern,—both officers bearing a commission from his Majesty. Their dresses, or uniforms, were made of grey dungaree piped with black, blue caps, and no shoes. They were well supplied with arms, such as rifles and double-barrel fowling pieces; the officers had swords. The men went through their drill and evolutions with great promptness and exactness. On their approaching the *whare* appointed to accommodate his Majesty, the party halted, and the guard formed an avenue, through which Matutaera passed on his entrance into the house.

After a short time the soldiers were dismissed to the quarters set aside for their use, and three sentries remained on duty for the first night (after which only two were posted); these were relieved at stated intervals, à la militaire.

Matutaera recognised me : sent for me ; and we had several interviews during his visit.

On another occasion, I saw the King at Rangiriri, at the time of the assemblage of Wiremu Kingi te Rangitakei. Hori te Kai-o-roto, and several other influential chiefs from the Southward, who had come to see Matutaera on business of state. They expressed their disapprobation of my reception, and of his familiarity with me : but, on his hearing of this, he informed them that he was king, and that I was an old friend of his deceased father.

After so much chat about war and politics, it is high time to introduce another subject,—that of love and matrimony.

In civilized countries the gentlemen often divide their love amongst favored belles ; but in New Zealand the favored belles have often been divided literally amongst their admirers. I have known a case in point, where two parties contended for the possession of a female ;—women and land, being, by the way, at the bottom of almost all inter-tribal wars; neither party, in this case, had the best of it, and so they went in for an application of Solomon's judgment, and they coolly each—took half ! not for the purpose of kai, but to prevent its being said that the one side had, after all, had the entire woman !

The female branch of a family are considered the property of the mother's tribe, who have the right to appropriate their labor, to betroth them or give them in marriage, as the case may be, the father hardly having a voice in the matter ; but in such marriages de convenance it has occurred that the lady had a secret lover. The knowledge of this sometimes coming to the ears of the betrothed husband's friends, they

would prepare to abduct her; but, on the other hand, the
lover's friends would also muster in his behalf, and the
result would be a regular case of "pull devil, pull baker!"
the lady being the chief sufferer in the operation. At the
beginning of such a struggle some little consideration might
be shown for decency; but, as they warmed to their work,
the girl would get completely stripped. Sometimes both
parties would be equal in strength, and a compromise would
be effected by the lover giving a consideration and obtaining
the lady. I have heard of a case where the lover's *taua* was
the strongest, and every probability existed of its being
successful in opposition to the wishes of the lady's relations,
when one of the latter sprung forward, tomahawk in hand,
exclaiming, "She shall not go with you alive; if you persist
in wanting her, you'll only get half!" And a few cuts with
the tomahawk on the body as it was being dragged almost
asunder by the two parties soon did the trick.

In the case of intestine war, it was not unusual when the
quarrel was of a serious nature, and where each party intended the extermination of the other, for a chief of the
attacking party to secure to himself portions of the enemy's
land by throwing a mat on the ground, sticking up a spear,
perhaps a *taiaha*, or probably turning up a small portion of
the soil as a *taunaha* to enforce his claim. I have heard of
considerable blocks of land having been secured by those
means and considered by the rest as inviolable; the rank of
the individual may have had some weight in the matter; at
all events the claim was respected, that is, provided that the
party attacked was vanquished.

The feeling of honor and respect of one chief to another
was often exhibited even in time of war. One case I will
mention out of many. At the commencement of the war
with the Europeans in the Waikato, the King party, finding
that a portion of the Ngatiteata tribe had remained loyal,

I

and that Aihipene Kaihau, the chief, had stayed with that
section, sent him word that they would not molest Waiuku,
his land. This promise they kept inviolate, though a serious
engagement took place at the Mauku, about eight miles from
Waiuku, between the volunteers (settlers) and Maories, in
which both sides suffered severely. The white force was
very small; the Maori party mustered more than three
hundred; and it is believed that the Mauku engagement was
the most dashing affair throughout the war on the part of
the Volunteers: had the information been attended to
which Waata Kukutai forwarded to the officer in command
at Waiuku, apprising him of a large body of natives having
crossed the river, the affair would have been rendered complete, as the force could have been strengthened, and the
attacking natives met in a manner to ensure their total defeat. As it was, the Europeans killed three Maories for
every one of their own party that fell, and that, notwithstanding their defeat and the loss of their officers.

I have before mentioned that only on one occasion have I
had a real quarrel in anger with a native, and I may as well
give the particulars, as they will serve to illustrate the pecu-
liarity of the Native's temperament, which can with the
most perfect hypocrisy disguise any ill feeling which may
exist, brood over a supposed injury, and bide its time for a
chance of taking vengeance for it. The man with whom I
had the row had really no cause for anger; but he was very
annoyed because when we left Waikato through fear of the
Ngapuhi I went to live with another tribe. This loss of his
"pakeha" (myself) touched his pride, and he determined some
day or another to pay me off. Years after my supposed de-
sertion from him I was living in the interior, at Toroakapakapa, and proud in the possession of a goose presented to me
by a very old friend who had taken it during the Waikato
raid on Tawatawhiti, described above. He fancied the cry

of the bird resembled my name, so it was reserved from slaughter, *tapued*, and given to me. It was the custom of native parties passing by my place to sit down to have a rest and look about; and of course their numerous dogs used to snuff around. One day, while some Maories were resting, a dog of theirs went after poor goosey, and pitched into it most unmercifully. It then walked into a pet pig of mine; and, as by this time I had got hold of my gun, I rolled it over dead as a stone. One of the natives—the very man just mentioned—came up to me, as I supposed, to claim my gun as *utu* for his dog; so I chucked the piece over into the garden, whereon my *friend* at once closed with me. I did not think there was much the matter, and I let him take an advantage which resulted in my going down, with him on the top of me. Being down, I thought my best plan was to be quiet and husband my strength, while my amiable savage was exerting himself to keep me down. Presently, he asked if I had had enough. Of course I would not grant this; and we rose and prepared for another tussle, in which I was determined not again to give such a chance as I had given before. We were wrestling on a bit of a flat about fifty or sixty feet above the river, the bank sloping pretty steeply down to the water's edge; so I got my friend close to the brink, by a sharp twist disengaged myself, at the same time giving him a "cross-leg," and down he went rolling head over heels flop into the stream. He came up well soused, and furious, and went away roaring vengeance, but did not try it on. He never has forgiven me, and I am sure he has not forgotten his douse.

The *tapu* of burial places in former times was generally strict, and any interference with them was always visited very severely on the offending parties; sometimes even with death, but always by the *muru*—*i. e.*, a general plunder of their goods and chattels, slaves being looked upon in the light of the latter. Often the innocent have suffered for the guilty, the usual custom being indiscriminate retaliation. One case, out of many, I will adduce. It was formerly the custom, and, indeed, still now obtains on certain occasions, that, when a chief of rank died, his remains were buried secretly in some place known only to the *tohungas* of the tribe, so that his enemies might not have the satisfaction of disinterring his bones in revenge for offences committed by him whilst in the flesh. A man of rank departed this life, and was accordingly interred with all due mystery. Some time afterwards it happened that his tribe had to leave the district, on account of some attack upon them, and did not return to it. Time passed on, and a family connected with the tribe, but of low rank, happening to journey through the country, lit accidentally upon the old chief's grave. They had suffered some injury at his hands, and this was a fine chance of paying him off: so they made fish-hooks out of his bones. This fearful desecration leaked out, and spread general indignation among the dead man's relations, who at once prepared for revenge. A *taua* was organized, came up with the offending party, and killed and ate the man and his wife; the children being made slaves.

PART II.

CHAPTER V.

Present Waikato.

I THINK it is Dr. Johnson who somewhere describes the delights of travelling in a postchaise, and expatiates on the pleasurable emotions experienced in gliding along good turnpike roads, past villages and hamlets, with no further trouble than paying the postboys at each stage. Had he lived in our day, he would probably have painted the comfort of a first-class *coupé*, inaccessible (thanks to a judicious "tip" to the guard) to any troublesome objector to tobacco. I do not know, however, that he could have brought himself to say much in favor of New Zealand coaches, constituted after the model of King Cobb; and, in default of railways, he would have been reduced to recommend the buggy and the saddle.

With both these modes of travelling through the northern island of New Zealand, as well as with a third—walking—it has been my luck to become tolerably familiar; and the scenes I have witnessed contrast so strongly with those described in "Waikato Forty Years Ago," that I have been tempted to tack my experiences on to that description. Where its writer found a country inhabited by thousands of natives, I saw cultivated farms, occupied by a thriving European population: where he wandered through difficult bush tracks, I drove along a metalled road; and where he witnessed deeds of savage slaughter, I met happy and contented English families, pursuing their daily avocations in peace and quiet.

I must confess to a partiality for the Waikato District, at least that portion of it south of Ngaruawahia; I like its country, its climate, and its scenery; and it is a matter of pleasure to me to mark on each successive visit signs of improvement, of increase in population, and of a general prosperous go-aheadedness.   Perhaps it was from having for a length of time lived in the Bay of Plenty, where surrounding hills gave one always the impression of being cooped up, that the rolling plain of the delta, not, however, quite destitute of mountain scenery, made so favorable an impression.   Here was a country over which one could ride in more than one or two directions; it was even possible to contemplate the existence of future fox-hounds or harriers, and some sport was to be obtained beyond wading waist-deep in mud and water after ducks.

My last visit was in the summer of this year; but, as I have stated in the preface, I have condensed in one recital the account of what I saw and heard during several trips.

We were four in number; the buggy was roomy; Cobb and Co. had furnished a very fair pair of horses; it was delightful summer weather, and we had plenty of time before us; so it was decided we should take two days to get to Ngaruawahia and look about us as we drove along.   For several miles after leaving Auckland the road runs through a level plain of volcanic soil, dotted with numerous cones, testifying to the extensive plutonic agency which in prehistoric times made the Auckland isthmus a centre of eruption. Ages upon ages elapsed, and when the first natives made their appearance, whenever that was, they found in these hills positions of great natural strength, of which they at once availed themselves; terraces were formed on the flanks, and tier upon tier of palisading arose. These have now all crumbled away, but the lines are still distinctly visible, and here and there can be found slight excavations, the sites of old *whares* or *ruas.* Now, the cones are turned to another use, and form quarries of scoria, whence is carted on to roads a "metal," which, at first highly detrimental to boots, eventually binds down into a firm, smooth highway. Past the "Harp of Erin," on either hand, the paddocks are littered with large blocks of the same material, and the plough can do but little; but surface-sown grass takes kindly to the red deposit, and herds of cattle roam amongst these relics of one of nature's fiercest convulsions. We passed by the upper waters of the Manukau harbour, the Heads sharp and distinct some twenty miles off; Onehunga, with the strong sunlight gleaming upon its houses, looking actually populous and pretty; and another mile brought us to Otahuhu, a quiet and dreamy-looking little village, rather altered since 1832.* Some water for the horses, a glass of beer for ourselves, and on we trundled again on the well-kept road, between thorn hedges, furze hedges, and post and rail fences, enclosing paddocks of splendid grass. There was joy among the graziers this season; the summer had afforded a good supply of rain, the grass was as green as in October, and the cattle were in tip-top condition. It was a treat to see the plain looking so well; and the contrast its cultivated surface presented with the dark bush-covered hills of the Hunua sloping down to it right in front of us was most pleasing to the eye. We passed Papatoetoe, where a crumbling mound on a rise shews the site of an old redoubt; and here, for some time, we left the good land behind us. From this for several miles the soil quite changes its condition, and becomes a cold clay of the poorest character, through which more than one stream brawls over a pebbly bed, out of which our sons will some day land the trout their fathers are introducing. We drove without stopping through Papakura, the site formerly

---

* page 30.

of a strong garrison, and the scene of several murders in the early days of the war; and, three miles further, halted for lunch at Drury. Otahuhu had looked dull; Papakura was not as lively as of yore: but it was not till alighting here that the difference between the past days of 1863 and the present could be realised. Then Drury was a scene of bustle and activity, full of officers and men of every branch of the service: of orderlies always at a gallop; of fussy brigade majors, and of all the pomp and paraphernalia of war. Now it was a desert; but if we missed the exciting sights of olden times, we also missed with gratitude the abomination which then formed the Drury soil: it was without exception the most yellow and sticky clay I ever sank into, as slippery as ice, and as tenacious as bird-lime. The 4th Division mud on the slopes of Cathcart Hill was bad enough, but it was a fool to this. Drury used to be a Brigadier's command, and the impetus given to it by the camp enabled an enterprising settler to cut up his property around it in lots, and sell at a price which, it is believed, astounded no one more than himself. It has not, however, leaked out that any of the purchasers have largely enriched themselves by that little speculation in land. Close by this are some disused coal mines: and on the summit of a wooded hill is still to be seen a dead tree which was once mistaken by an enthusiastic camp-adjutant for native enemies in white blankets. I need scarcely add that there was considerable chaff on the return of the force sent out to reconnoitre. After quitting Drury the country again improves as the road rises over the Hunua ranges, passing over Razorback and Pokeno hills, through bush which ten years ago was traversed by a narrow track, but which now has receded far back before the axe of the settler. Almost all traces have disappeared of the redoubts and stockades which were formerly thought necessary for the safety

of convoys, and pleasant-looking farm-houses, with here
and there a small church or a school-house, nestle in the
hollows or stand out by the road side. It is still a steepish
pinch over Pokeno hill, the range which parts the Auckland
basin from that of Waikato, and from its summit we got the
first view of the river, flowing apparently straight to where
we stood, an intervening height hiding the deflexion to the
westward which the nature of the hills on the northern
bank forces it to adopt. It was a fine panorama : ahead lay
the basin of Middle Waikato, through which the broad
stream was winding its course between dark clumps of white
pines or sedgy banks : in the furthest distance a range of
hills ran across the horizon, the peak of Taupiri denoting
the position of the pass through which the river finds its
way from the delta : to the westward was bush, and
seemingly nothing but bush, traversed not so long ago by
merely a few native tracks, but now rapidly disappearing
as the settler creates a home for his family, or the railway
contractor pushes on his embankment : eastward was
swamp, bounded by the Piako hills ; and behind us, the
inland waters of the Manukau, and the smiling country
through which we had passed. At the foot of the Pokeno
hill extended a large swamp, the exhalations from which
produce a curious scene in the early morning. Standing at
such a time on this summit, no sign of the plain appears :
all is thick fog, curling so high up the flanks of the adjacent
hills that only their tops are to be seen, and the spectator
can almost fancy himself looking down upon some placid,
milk-white sea, whose waters wash the bases of numerous
islets. Forty miles from Auckland we reached the Mangatawhiri Creek, the passage of which by General Cameron's
troops in 1863 led to the action of Koheroa, fought on the
low range skirting the southern bank. Throughout our
journey we had passed continuous heaps of earth, remains of

K

redoubts erected when, notwithstanding a force of some 10,000 men in the field, it was unsafe for small parties to travel along the road; and, close to Mangatawhiri, were the *débris* of the largest, Queen's redoubt. Many a spot, the scene of a skirmish, reminded us of good and brave fellows who had lost their lives in a warfare destitute of glory. At Otahuhu was seen the obelisk erected to the memory of that gallant gentleman, Colonel Nixon; there was the Drury monument to Percival and Norman, and the men who fell with them at Mauku; the old camping ground near it was full of reminiscences of the two Hunters; Shepherd's Bush recalled the cheery aspect of Ring, killed in a vain attempt to carry Orakau by storm: it seemed only the other day that Booth and his 43rd marched into Drury, astonishing all beholders by their scarlet patrol jackets, which contrasted so disparagingly with the ragged blue serge attire of officers coming from the front. Trevor and Phelps, of the 14th, and Mercer, of the Artillery, once more held the Queen's Redoubt; and the memory of many a hearty laugh enjoyed at mess with men whose fate has since been a soldier's grave gave a sombre tint to every recollection by the way. About a mile after crossing the Mangatawhiri, skirting the Koheroa hills along a road constructed through a dismal swamp, the Waikato river was reached: a broad stream, running between low sedgy banks backed up by fern and cabbage trees, and bearing here on its bosom small islets, in other words, over-grown sand-banks. This spot is Mercer, the proposed terminus, for the present, of the Auckland-Waikato Railway, the works of which have more than once crossed our road. This railway is the thought by day and the dream by night of nine-tenths of the Waikato settlers. They want it right up to Ngaruawahia; they have made up their minds to have it, and until it is obtained they are not likely to give much peace to the powers that be.

At Mercer we stopped for the night, taking a swim in the river, which we soon found had a current against which it was hard work to make way. It is a pity to see a fine stream like this, with a width varying from 150 yards, almost useless from its shallowness, its snags, and the continuous shifting of its sand banks. None but steamers of the smallest draught navigate its waters, and these are of a miserable description; but it needs only the increase of agriculture in the Waikato plains and the development of the coal and lime resources known to exist in the ranges to create, pending the construction of the railway, a fleet of vessels built expressly for the purpose, combining with light draught the power to stem a strong current.

From Mercer a baddish piece of road, fascine made, runs between the river and the skirting hills; and a mile or two of it brought us to the southern slope of Koheroa, at the foot of which flows the Whangamarino stream, and from whose summit Pickard's 40-pounders used to drop occasional shells into the Meremere pa, two miles further; presently we ascended a small rise and we were at Meremere itself, before which General Cameron halted for weeks, only to find it evacuated when **he made a** turning movement by the river. From this, the country is dreariness itself; to the left there lies a huge swamp, extending apparently right up to the distant hills which separate the Waikato basin from that of the Thames. On the right are caught rare glimpses of the river, and the sole growth around consists of dwarf fern or titree. Fifteen miles of this bleak travelling, **and on** rising a slope we saw on one hand Waikari Lake, on the other, the Waikato; and in front, on the narrow strip of land between the two, Rangiriri (angry sky), a small spot of ground, but hallowed by the memory of those who fell at the rash and disastrous assault on the pa, when linesmen, artillery, and sailors had to recoil with heavy loss before the fire poured upon them from the formidable and unbreached fortification they were ordered to storm.

Some time ago a friend of mine was standing on the ruins of these works in company with a chief who had taken a leading part in the defence. "Here it was," said the native, "that I stripped for the fight; and there is the spot where I buried one hundred sovereigns, wrapped up in my blue shirt. I cannot touch that money now; my people cannot; it is *tapu* from the blood which has been shed here." I doubt if every European to whom this tale might have been related would have been so scrupulous as my friend: I fear that in most cases the *tapu* would have speedily been broken. From Rangiriri to Rahui-Pokeka the country begins to improve, and right in front rises a chain of wooded hills, one of whose peaks is Taupiri, the old burial place of Waikato chiefs, and *tapu* to such an extent that none but funeral parties were formerly allowed to pass along its flank. Ordinary travellers had to cross the river and take to the other side; but as Molière's doctor says, "We have changed all that," and Cobb's coach rolls on at its foot quite unobservant of the sacredness of the spot. Rahui-Pokeka consists of a small inn and a few fenced paddocks, and nearly opposite, on the other bank, a long wooden shoot denotes the locality of the Kupakupa coal mine, which, thanks to the manager's kindness, we were going to visit. After crossing, we climbed up a hill for a short distance, walked through a tunnel where the coal had first been discovered, and worked afterwards by the Imperial troops, then along a short tramway in the open and entered a black vault. There was no putting on of miners' dresses, or going down by the "man-engine." We simply took each a candle, and blundered on in the darkness. Presently the eye got accustomed to the gloom, and we were able to make out our surroundings. We were simply in a vault of coal; the arched roof above us extending in a straight line for about a hundred yards without a single support was seventeen feet in height; the side walls were twenty feet apart, and the whole was coal, resting on fire-clay of superior quality. The manager told us that the seam was still several feet thick overhead, and that it extended to some depth below our feet. Then we went on, and saw the miners at work; and, through a narrow gallery, emerged again into the open, only to see another drive straight in front in the opposite face of a small ravine. This was also entered, and examined; and we got an idea of the value of the mine when we learnt that the seam had been struck seven miles inland. The coal is of tertiary formation, and does very well for the river steamers and for house purposes: but, like everybody in Waikato, the manager grumbled hugely at the want of a railway which would enable him to deliver it at decent prices in Auckland. In addition to the coal and fire-clay there is a brick field close at hand, which turns out very good bricks. The nuisance about the place is that the river bed is always shifting; for instance, underneath the shoot where the previous year ample water existed for the steamers, there was at the time of our visit a depth of only two feet. I have only one suggestion to make with regard to the mine, and this I hope the manager will take in good part, as it is given purely with regard to the danger he must constantly run of being drowned or drowning others: that he should induce the company to expend a small part of their profits in the purchase of a boat. I may never have to cross here again, but if I do, I trust it may not be in the ricketty flat-bottomed punt produced on this occasion. The current was no joke, the wobbling qualities of the cockle-shell were in inverse ratio to her steering powers, and complete immobility was our only chance. It was all very well, in answer to our expressions of disquiet, to learn that there were only two feet of water under us, except in the channel : but, how if one upset *in* the channel ? Anyhow, a spill anywhere would not have been comfortable.

A drive of some nine more miles along the flanks of Taupiri and thence through a bit of level country, brought us in good time to the old Maori King's capital, Ngaruawahia,* where we crossed the Horotiu in a punt, this time a wire-worked one and tolerably safe.

During the whole of this trip of about ninety miles we had not come upon a single native on our side of the river. On the other bank an occasional hamlet was seen, and now and then a canoe darted from under the bushes, going against the stream in apparently the easiest possible manner. They were, however, but few and far between, the whilom possessors of the land all around us, and chiefly belonged to *hapus* (sub-tribes), which took the European side during the war, and have been located on part of the confiscated lands to the west of the Waikato River.

Situated at the confluence of two rivers whose union forms Waikato proper, the **Waipa** and the Horotiu, the latter proceeding from the snows of Ruapehu and in its course traversing the inland sea of Taupo, Ngaruawahia forms the apex of the delta which is considered Upper Waikato. Here ends the sterile land, and for miles upwards the soil, composed of a fluviatile deposit mixed with the pulverised scoria ejected from the central volcanoes, improves rapidly. All throughout there is a gradual rise ; the plateau of Taupo, where the pumice sand precludes all nutritious vegetation, forming the background of the view.

We found here the usual hotels and stores, but in addition there were local industries in the shape of a flax (Phormium tenax) and flour mill, a newspaper office, and a brewery, in

* The "a" as in the French "la." The whole as Narwawaya.

combination with which was a pleasant hop garden, reminding a home-sick colonist of many a jolly ride through
Kentish hop grounds. One marvel of ingenuity, which,
alas! no longer exists, was formerly proudly shewn as a
proof of the scientific skill of the Staff College, being a
redoubt erected by a member of that learned body (specially
detached for the purpose from higher duties) for the
reception of the women and children of the district in case of
attack from the interior. It was constructed with such a
regard to the principles of fortification, and with such
consideration for flanking fire, that its linear defence would
have required about four times the number of men the area
could have held, and the parapets were built up with sods
perpendicularly on the edge of a small stream. The consequence was that one dark night a heavy rain pouring down
on the soft soil converted the rivulet into a ravine and
carried off one entire face; the rest quietly crumbled away,
to the delight of the officer commanding the district. It is
now replaced by a red-brick square building, which looks
like a miniature jail gone blind, and which competes in
ugliness with a wooden mausoleum close at hand, erected by
the Maories over the grave of Potatau, their first King, the
father of Matutaera or Tawhiao, the reigning monarch.
There must have been goodly changes of level here, for the
ravine scooped out near the block-house, or whatever it is
called, reveals the fact that at a depth of some feet below the
surface lie imbedded the remains of a forest, the stumps of
which are still standing, and are chiefly *totara*,* a tree which
does not now grow in Waikato. It did not take long to
see the lions of Ngaruawahia, and the next morning we
were *en route* for Hamilton. It was all level now, and easy
work for the horses. To the right we had a long range of
hills bordering the western bank of the Waipa, and extending

* Podocarpus Totara.

till they culminated in Mount Pirongia, near Alexandra; in front rose a large detached mountain, Mangatautari, beyond Cambridge; and, far to the left, was a continuation of the same ridges we had seen during the last day's drive.

Hamilton, prettily situated on the Horotiu, acts as the metropolis of Waikato, the head-quarters of the Constabulary, &c.; and here we obtained horses, and rode on by Ohaupo to Alexandra on the Waipa, along a very fair road constructed partly by Road Boards, partly by Constabulary labour. As far as Hamilton we had seen but few traces of habitation and farming, but now we were entering a country which is rapidly being taken up, and which bids fair to become not only populous, but also prosperous. One of the very first things which strikes the visitor in Waikato is the quantity of good land lying idle; and to any question on the subject the same answer is almost always given, " Oh ! it's military settlers' land." Notably in one instance is this exemplified, and that is in the country between Ngaruawahia and Alexandra, on the right bank of the Waipa. There are to be found thousands of acres, formerly supporting a large native population and producing corn in abundance, which have once more returned to a wild state. After confiscation they were allotted to military settlers, who sold them for mere songs to speculative buyers, who do not now well know what to do with them; especially as, when the purchasers can be found, they are sharply pounced upon by Road Boards for rates. In the twenty-five or thirty miles ridden over really good country when I took that journey I do not remember having seen a dozen settlers; but that was some two years ago, and an improvement may have taken place—though I have not heard of any.

In every settlement where the plan was adopted of granting lands on a quasi-military tenure, the same unhappy result is found. Men without the taste or experience for a farmer's life, and **mostly** quite devoid of capital, received a grant of fifty or more acres, of as much use to them as if they were in the moon. Some of the men utilised them to pay off small grog scores; others sought a market in Auckland, where they obtained only nominal prices; some held on in hopes of good times and increased value; a few set to work manfully on their little properties; while by good fortune others disposed of their lands to enterprising and real settlers who, whilst cultivating to their own **advantage**, are also largely benefiting the district. To this state of things there are but two remedies. Either the evil will cure itself as immigration progresses and as present holders are induced to sell the unremunerative lands they possess, or else the **Government will have** itself to become the purchaser wherever **possible,** and retail the property thus acquired to the immigrants they introduce, or throw it generally into **the market.** The latter course would be the speediest means of altering the present desolate aspect of many **a fertile** tract of country which now lies idle and useless. Whether it be practicable is another question.

After getting **on the** Ohaupo road we **found numerous** signs of cultivation; considerable tracts of land were **well in** grass, carefully fenced **and amply stocked;** and more than once we were pointed out estates owned by gentlemen of position and wealth who have made the Waikato their home, and who are **busy** improving properties destined to become most valuable.

Part **of the** way was through rather **low** ground, but from the rises we could see **that** all the surface water would **run into** a number **of small** lakes lying at a sufficient level above the Waipa **to ensure** good drainage.

Ohaupo was originally a German settlement, colonised by the members of that nation who formed a company in the

Waikato Militia, and some miles after leaving it we reached
Paterangi, a formidable position on a saddle taken up by
the natives in 1864 to bar the progress of the troops. So
strong was it, that, with the experience of Rangiriri fresh in
his mind, General Cameron, who was marching up the
Waipa, did not care about attacking it, but turned it by a
flank movement, which led to the fight of Rangiawhia.
There was, however, close by it a dashing little affair in a
bit of scrub, out of which the Colonial Forces came out
with no little *kudos*. From this hill we could see some two
miles off the township of Alexandra, our destination, nest-
ling, as it were, under the shadow of Mount Pirongia, and
traversed by the deep-banked and sluggish Waipa, spanned
by a good bridge; beyond it rose a solitary cone,
Kakepuke, which should from its appearance, be all that is
left of an extinct volcano ; and to the left, more and more
substantial houses and cultivations filled the view till the
latter was closed by the low ridge of Rangiawhia.

We crossed the Mangapiko, a tortuous affluent of the
Waipa, on a good bridge near the mouth, and riding past
a pretty new church and a Constabulary station arrived at
the hotel, which faced Pirongia.

From the windows are to be seen the bare spurs the
mountain sends down from its bushy summit, and the very
spot can be almost perceived where in 1870 Mr Todd was
shot while surveying land for a friendly Maori chief: the
only premeditated and quasi-political murder, and not
resulting from personal quarrel, which has been committed
by a King native upon a white man in Waikato since the
close of the war.* There is no doubt that this assassination
was caused, like so many Maori inter-tribal wars, by land :
and that a grievance on this subject, rankling in the minds
of individuals, led them to perpetrate the atrocity : in their

* Vide note at end of chapter.

subsequent conduct the leaders of the King party, who had
no hand in the murder, acted very much like the peasantry
in disturbed parts of Ireland, who, though blaming an
assassin, think it a point of honour, or patriotism, or what
not, to shelter him.   Consequently, the murderers are still
at large.   In common with every colonist who has at heart
the true interests of the country, the Waikato settlers are
unanimous in their desire for peace : there is among them
a total absence of that enmity of race which is so often
displayed where the white man and the coloured meet on the
frontier, and which leads to "bead-drawing" and savage
reprisals.   War means for them farms abandoned before
marauding parties, lands lying waste, homesteads in flames,
and the substitution of harassing military service for the
industrial pursuits by which their district is advancing in
prosperity.   If any party of men in the colony clamours for
what are called "vigorous measures" against the King
natives, so long as these as a body remain quiet it is
certainly not that most interested in the matter, the settlers
on the frontier.

The general feeling appears to be that all danger would
be at an end were it a settled thing that the perpetrators of
outrages such as Mr. Todd's murder should be given up to
justice whenever they take refuge in the haunts over which
the Maori King claims to govern ; and that, once this rule
established, Tawhiao might go on as long as he liked with
his mimicry of reigning.   Till then, however, there is always
the chance, remote or not as may be, and certainly
diminishing every day, of the extreme section of the
Kingites, in whatever minority it may be, repeating such
deeds with a view to forcing its more peaceably-inclined
brethren into another conflict, which would be undertaken
on our part under far different conditions from those in
force during the late wars.   Then the interior was almost a

terra incognita; in the centre and on both coasts our hands
were full; and in our marches we had to trust to whatever
information could be picked up about tracks. Now we have
good roads up to the frontier ; on the east coast the
turbulent mountain tribes have been brought into submission ; on the west the lingering spirit of disaffection is
confined to a small section ; in the centre only is to be
found anything like cohesion among the malcontents ;
and, in addition to this, we know the country. Of
these facts the Kingites are as well aware as we are,
and they must see that a rising on their part would lead
to their inevitable ruin. That such a contingency may
never occur is the ardent hope of every settler, in the
interests of the colony as well as those of humanity ; for,
to use a paraphrase which has been employed before, the
very worst use you can put a Maori to, is to shoot him ; not
forgetting that there is just as good a probability of his
shooting you. Holding this opinion, I could not quite
agree with an American gentleman I once met in the South
who was giving me some of his experiences in the Far
West, in the course of which he made use of the expression,
"good Indians."   I supposed he meant "friendlies ;" but
his answer disabused me very soon. "No, sir," he said;
"you see, sir, with us, all *good* Indians are just there, sir,
there," and the emphatic manner in which he pointed to
the ground showed pretty plainly that he considered
that goodness and life could not co-exist in an Indian.
My western friend's platform was evidently the "d—d
nigger" policy, one which will never do for New Zealand,
and which General Grant very soon got rid of in America.
The first place of interest we visited was the angle at the
confluence of the Waipa and Mangapiko, where formerly
stood the Matatitaki pa, whose destruction by the Ngapuhi
is related at page 15. It was difficult to believe that where

we stood, within the fenced paddock of the Constabulary,
with a church to one hand, a steamer alongside the bank to
the other, a good bridge across the river, houses and gardens
around us, and the English flag flying close by, only a few
short years ago the Maories were assembled in thousands.
Where were they now? There were certainly a few
knocking about: their occupation was selling turkeys, and
kits of peaches; but where were the descendants of the
warriors who cultivated the broad plain of the delta, and
who were found formerly in such numbers along the banks
of the Waipa? The *friendly* natives of the entire Waikato,
from its mouth upwards, assembled to bid farewell to Sir
G. Bowen in March 1873, amounted to only about six
hundred men; the Kingite Waikato may muster about
seven or eight hundred; Ngatimaniapoto probably as many,
and that is all remaining out of a large population. Inter-
tribal strife, disease, the adoption of new habits, clothing,
and food, spirits, and war with the European are the causes
which have thus decreased their numbers. Not in Waikato
alone, but in every other part of the Island is the same
result to be observed. Riding along the shores of the Bay
of Plenty and of the East Coast one sees a succession of
old pas, testifying to a formerly abundant population, now
sadly diminished; and it is impossible not to feel regret that
a race which has given so many proofs of its adaptability to
a higher standard should thus disappear bit by bit.

Some two years ago I was at Alexandra during a native
meeting, when a tribe named the Ngatiraukawa, who in-
habit the right bank of the Waikato, from Taupo to
Cambridge, intimated to the representatives present of the
King natives that all connection between them, in a political
point of view, was at an end. Each party was drawn up
on the opposite banks of a short hollow road, and talked to
each other pretty plainly. But we were very disappointed

in the chief speaker on the part of Ngatiraukawa. What he ought to have done was this. He should have stalked out gravely, his head adorned with feathers, a mat round his waist, another on his shoulders, and a *taiaha* (spear) in his hand. Selecting a piece of ground about ten or fifteen yards long, he should have started from the one end and pranced up to the other, pouring forth rapidly his utterances, and emphasizing them by gestures and contortions of the body: arriving at the further end, a jump or two, accompanying some telling point, should have concluded a sentence, whereon he ought to have retraced his steps quietly to his starting point and begun again. But these people were evidently degenerate: they were dressed in European clothing; they stood up and talked to each other as if they were hon. members assembled in Parliament; there was no "taki-ing" up and down; no screaming out arguments in a state of frantic excitement; there was not half the row there would be at a Road Board meeting; and yet the interview was of tolerable importance, being neither more nor less than an avowal of defection from the King's authority by a tribe which had hitherto adhered to his side. During this very stay at Alexandra there was some little excitement about the opening up of the supposed Tuhua goldfield in the King country, and a friend we met told us he had been once rather sanguine on the subject. After talking in vain to natives, he came across a "Pakeha-Maori" (*i.e.*, an European who has lived for a length of time among the natives), who with many mysterious nods gave him to understand that he knew all about it. Of course our friend set to work pumping him, and "shouted" liberally till the old fellow's tongue was unloosed. Now, my friend was ready to swallow a good deal; a report of a reef likely to yield a couple of hundred ounces to the ton would not have frightened him: but when his informant gave him to

understand he had seen solid layers of gold in the rocks, and
when he found out that this "truthful James" had never been
near the spot described, he quietly stopped the supply of
liquor and dropped the acquaintance. While exploring the
lions of the neighbourhood, places all known in connection
with the late war, we rode over the confiscation boundary
into the native territory, feeling very much like school-boys
out of bounds. I am not quite sure that some of the party
were not prepared at any turn in the path to hear the war
shout, and find ourselves encircled by an ambuscade of grim
savages, armed to the teeth, and eager to avenge on our
unhappy persons the wrongs sustained at the hands of our
countrymen. We did not see any ambuscade ; we saw one
armed aboriginal, and his weapon was an eel-spear. He was
even friendly, and said " *tena-koe*"* to each of the party, and
then he went on his way singing—no, not singing : there
ought to be a word coined to express the hideous row the
Maori makes when harmony is in him ; it isn't singing ; it
isn't grunting ; and it isn't exactly howling—but it's a neat
combination of all three, with uncommonly little of the first
element in it. I have heard of seeing spiders and seeing
snakes ; but at Kopua, a small village some three or four
miles beyond the boundary, in old times a mission station,
we saw eels : big eels, and little eels ; eels as long as my arm
and nearly as thick ; eels as long as my leg, only not quite
as thick ; eels that looked as if half a dozen of them could
digest any one of us very easily, and consequently most
grewsome eels ; and these were not in dozens, but in
hundreds. There was to be a great meeting in a few days ;
some visitors were to pass through on their way up or
down, and a haul had been made in the marshes lying at the
foot of the conical and extinct-volcano-like knoll, some six
or seven miles off. Talking of Kakapuke, we heard at

---

* How are you ?—lit., there you are.

Alexandra that some time ago a native brought into the settlement a lump of virgin copper : of course, everybody wanted to know where this came from, and the owner was shouted for enthusiastically : eventually our informant was selected as the confidant, and he and a friend started with the native to climb Kakapuke, on whose flanks the ore was said to have been found. It need not be said how during the walk they arranged the future company, settled who were to have preference shares, and what number, and what capital they would name to start the mine, &c., &c. They left off talking when they got to the first raupo swamp : that was damp and unpleasant : then came another and another, so that by the time they reached the actual foot of the hill they were mud and water up to the waist. They searched first one spot, then another ; then they went round, dived into every gully, and strained their eyes to catch the first glimpse of the lump from which the native finder declared he had knocked off his specimen. Not a sign of it was apparent : the wretched guide could not remember the exact spot. I have since learned that questions put to these two explorers on the subject of prospecting for copper do not possess a soothing influence.

The boundary of confiscation as laid down by Proclamation divides the lands cultivated by settlers who hold from the Crown from those still in the hands of the Kingite natives : of these latter, however, a good number of acres have been leased by Europeans. Still, the line answers somewhat to the system of the "Pale" in force in Ireland centuries ago, the exact Maori translation of which is *aukati*. An *aukati* is an imaginary line, defined by localities, across which the tribes or persons on whose account it is declared must not pass ; should they do so, it is at their own risk. In this case the confiscation line is not treated exactly as an *Aukati* by the natives, because they still harp upon the idea mentioned at page 57, that the Mangatawhiri creek, near Mercer, is the real northern boundary of their territories; or by the Europeans, as it is not quite in accordance with English customs of the present day to shoot a man, simply because he goes beyond a particular spot. Yet it has acquired a sort of importance, and a tacit acknowledgment that to the southward of it we have no business.

While at Alexandra we had the pleasure of an introduction to a chief whose family history gives a hint as to how his ancestors honoured their fathers : this is what was told us on the subject. His grandfather was a man of mild manners, blessed with rather an impetuous son. A neighbouring tribe happened to take some liberties with his crops, or horses, or wives, it is immaterial which, and the young man urged an expedition to chastise the aggressors. Faithful to his peace-principles, the aged chief besought him to calm himself, resolutely declined to have a hand in the fray, prophesied disaster, and winked at his son's going off with the best men of the tribe. Success attended the party ; and, returning laden with booty and prisoners, the son met his venerable father, who was standing at the *Waharoa* (principal gate of the pa), no doubt casting longing glances on the bipeds he deemed himself destined to chew. In his oiliest accents he praised his heroic boy on the valour and talent displayed, and congratulated him on the well-deserved laurels he had gained : but, instead of bending his head and meekly receiving his father's blessing, the young leader stormed : " You, indeed ! Why, you wouldn't come with us ! You wouldn't help us ! And now you butter us up !! You, why you're not fit to live !" And he shot the old gentleman dead.

. Another anecdote, but this time of conjugal attachment, was related to us one evening. An elderly Maori lady of high lineage, possessing some land near Auckland, was

M

espoused by—Bill Smith,—say. After living some time
together, they received a pressing invitation to visit Tokan-
gamutu, the King's head-quarters, and accepted it. Arrived
there, the wife was taken to a whare, and Smith was
quietly informed he had been guilty of presumption in
allying himself to royal blood, and that the marriage was
dissolved. By way of compensation, however, some damsels
were trotted out, of which Bill was allowed his pick. A
short time elapsed, and Bill, wandering on the outskirts of
the Waikato settlements, got into trouble about a saddle and
other small things he had found in a whare during the
owner's absence, and he was duly sent to Auckland jail.
The new spouse at once repudiated the connection : not so
with the old one ; she found her way to Auckland and
prayed hard for a daily interview with her husband. The
request was granted, and the warders' hearts used to melt as
from their posts they saw that her feelings were so over-
powering as to necessitate her throwing a blanket over her
husband's head and her own while she " tangi'd." The
cunning old lady knew her darling loved tobacco, and that
the rules forbad it, so every day she had her pipe ready,
and, while she wailed over her imprisoned spouse, he,
quietly secured by the blanket, managed to enjoy regularly his
morning smoke. The reader will be gratified to learn that
her love met with due reward and that they are now
believed to be living together, a picture of conjugal felicity.

Eight miles east of Alexandra is situated Te Awamutu,
formerly a large mission station, then General Cameron's
head-quarters, and now a small village situated in country
which is considered the cream of the Waikato. My notions
on the subject of farming are excessively vague, but even I
could appreciate the rich luxuriance of the soil, and join in
the praises which I heard showered upon it. From an
utilitarian point of view nothing could be finer than such

farms as were seen about Te Awamutu and Rangiawhia, and one near Kihikihi deserves mention for the elegance and tasteful care displayed by the owner on his plantations and garden. Wheat and oats, I was informed, answer capitally in this soil; as regards potatoes, I could judge for myself; and as for melons, pumpkins, *et hoc genus omne*, they were a drug in the market and rotting in the ground. Again there was growling about the railway which, when constructed, is to carry away to Auckland the produce now useless to the farmer.

Just beyond Te Awamutu comes a slight rise, forming a narrow saddle, on which stood two churches; one, Church of England; the other, Roman Catholic. As there is one of the former creed at Alexandra and another at Te Awamutu, it cannot be said that the district lacks buildings for worship. In the Rangiawhia church, now falling fast into decay, is a very handsome stained glass window, which contrasts rather strongly with the dilapidated state of the edifice it adorns; it is just as if an individual with a very seedy coat, hat, and trousers had on at the same time a brilliantly coloured new waistcoat.

Once at Rangiawhia we were on classic ground, as here it was General Cameron after his flank march round Paterangi came upon the unexpecting enemy, and a skirmish ensued which is still regarded by the natives in the light of a treacherous attack. They did not consider it fair that he should have left unassailed the position they had taken up expressly for fighting, and that he should appear suddenly in their rear. Some women unfortunately were accidentally shot during the affair, and of this they have made the most. A depression in the road still marks the site of a *whare* whence came the bullet which wounded mortally Colonel Nixon while he was humanely persuading its inmates to come out and surrender,

It was at Orakau, not far beyond this, that a determined band of natives, chiefly Uriwera, endured for three days the torments of hunger and thirst, to every summons to surrender answering, "We will fight "*Ake, ake, ake*" (for ever), and eventually broke through the investing force, with fearful loss to themselves.

From Rangiawhia one gets a very fairish view. To either hand, enclosing the plain and running on the further side of the rivers, are hills of respectable size; to the north, others surmounted by the holy peak of Taupiri close the view; southward the land ascends gradually and low mountain chains arise: and, on a fine day, two milk-white specks, just showing over the furthest ranges and looking at the first glance like fleecy clouds, are pointed out as the summits of Tongariro and Ruapehu. The confiscation boundary is not far off, and beyond it lies an undulating plain, equal in fertility to the soil around us, but covered all with fern; for the nearest Hau Hau cultivations to the frontier are at Aratitaha and Wharepapa, about five miles off. Close by, to the east, a dark belt of Kahikatea bush hid from us the Moana-tua-tua swamp, and through it we rode to see the works in progress for a road to Cambridge. At present to get to that place from any of the western settlements one has to ride back to Ohaupo, and then turn southward again, so that a direct track across the marsh will cause a saving of seventeen miles from Rangiawhia. The constabulary were hard at work, draining, fascining, and forming the road; the side ditches were from six to ten feet wide cut through a black spongy soil, more like peat than anything I have elsewhere met in the Island; and imbedded in this, and underlying the present Kahikatea bush, were stumps and logs of totara and matai, trees now unknown in the district, so tough as to defy the axe, and black as bog-oak. The work had so far advanced that we were able to walk across the narrow part selected as the shortest direction for the road. The swamp is really the property of private individuals, who purchased it from Government, and who are devoting a large amount of energy, labour, and capital to reclaiming it. It will pay somebody eventually, for the peat which comes out of it, after lying exposed to the air, crumbles away into very rich soil, and the amount of ditching done by the Constabulary assists the drainage materially. Another day was spent in knocking about Kihikihi and Orakau. With us was a friend who had been present at the fight, but even with his guidance the eye could barely trace the old Maori parapet. A fence ran along what had been one face, the remainder had crumbled away; and sheep were quietly nibbling the grass on this, the spot where the last stand was made by the natives in Waikato.

At a farm-house not far off, close to the boundary line, we got a wrinkle which might have been of use to Rarey, and which proved that our public school system of imparting education à tergo is applicable to horses as well as to boys.

Our host proposed a ride over the confiscation line, and went out into a paddock to catch a horse. There were about half-a-dozen of these at the furthest end, and no sooner had he begun to crack his whip, than the whole lot deliberately trotted up to him, just like dogs whistled to heel, and allowed themselves to be bridled. It seems that a judicious application of thong to them when young—care being taken never to strike them on the forehand—induces them to turn their heads towards the crack of the whip.

While going over Major Jackson's splendid farm, I was much puzzled by the appearance presented by a number of kahikatea stumps, standing in a swampy hollow near his house, and all about the same height, as if they had been cut down on purpose to the one level. I

had seen the remains of a forest mowed down by an
avalanche which had left the stumps in a very much
similar condition; but an avalanche theory would not do
for Waikato, so I left off conjecturing, and asked questions.
It was very simple after all. Years ago there grew on this
spot a bit of swampy bush through which ran a small
rivulet: this latter was dammed up by the natives to make
an eel-weir, the consequence being that a pond was formed,
the water attaining the height of the dam, and keeping to
that. The trees died; the part exposed to the air decayed
and fell, while that under water remained sound. When
the troops came up the embankment was broken, the pond
was emptied, and there now remain—a swamp, and the
puzzling stumps.

We were now in the country of pheasants; and, perhaps,
a slight sporting digression may not be amiss. It has constantly been asserted that there is no such thing as sport in
New Zealand, duck and pigeon shooting excepted. Neither
of these are certainly very amusing; as wading through
mud flats, and oftener crawling along them to get a chance
at the wily *Parera*, is very trying to the temper; while
sitting under a tree waiting for the pigeons to come to it
(the very best way to make a bag) is only another name for
going to sleep. But the pheasant has been introduced, and it
has propagated itself in the most wonderful manner; about
Auckland the birds are pretty well kept down; but in out-
districts they are to be found in abundance. I remember
once riding from Ohaupo to Cambridge at dawn, and being
astonished at the numbers I saw on the road side, apparently
perfectly tame and fearless: with a stock whip I could have
made a decent bag; but, that afternoon I went out with a
gun, and it was very different then; they were as wild as
hawks, strong on the wing, and devils to run. Once they
got into standing ti-tree, of course they were safe. The

natives beyond the boundary complain bitterly of them, and look upon them as the last pest introduced by that pestiferous individual, the pakeha. The Maori has no notion of shooting flying, even had he the ammunition, and so he growls out that his crops are destroyed, the very potatoes being scraped out of the ground when planted. For the matter of that, many an European does the same, not only with regard to pheasants, but also to all acclimatised birds; but we have not yet got quite as far as a "Sparrow Club."

In places like the Napier lagoons, where one can go about in a punt, the duck shooting is very fine sport; and I have seen more than one good bag of curlew (a capital bird for the table) made at Tauranga: were I to state the number brought down on one occasion with two barrels by an officer of the 68th, I could scarcely expect to be credited.

For a long time I was under the impression that no river fish existed in New Zealand which would take the fly. I had had many a tussle in Tauranga harbour with *kahawai*, a salt water fish in shape not unlike a salmon, which takes greedily a gaudy fly with plenty of white about it; but I was surprised to learn that the Waikato, at Cambridge, affords very fair sport. Fish have been killed there some three pounds in weight. Now, a three pound trout on a light rod in a Kerry stream gives no end of fun, and the river at Cambridge is rocky and rapid enough in all conscience. The fish is a kind of bull-headed trout; but, why it should be found here in goodly numbers, and not elsewhere, is certainly puzzling.

While at Alexandra we took a walk to Pirongia, intending to have a search for a seam of coal which had been found on its flanks; but somehow or another we missed the precise ravine; and blundering about in tall fern for some time being voted too hard work, we started home, and went to take a look at the rapids mentioned in page 17: it was

lucky we had been told there were rapids at that spot, else
we certainly should never have discovered their existence.
The coal we had missed is described as being of the same
kind as at the Taupiri mines, tertiary, and quite fit for house
purposes, &c. If worked, it would enable the settlers to
procure lime easily enough, as the formation of the Pirongia
ranges and of most of the hills stretching away to Raglan is
limestone.   From Alexandra we rode back to Hamilton, and
the next day, crossing the Horotiu by a sound self-propelling
punt, got on to the Cambridge road.   What has already
been said of other parts of the Waikato applies very
much to this portion of it.   That it possesses good soil
is evinced by the number of farms on it, some of them held
on lease from natives who have here extensive reservations ;
and that the owners are satisfied is proved by the absence
among them of the proverbial trait of the British farmer—
grumbling.   I am wrong, though ; there is one thing they
do grumble about, and of course it is the absence of a
railway.

Away from Hamilton eastward towards the Piako and the
Thames valley lies a large extent of swamp, and to the
northward of this again a fair amount of good country is
reported to exist.   Not satisfied with having their Auckland
railway begun, the settlers want a line running through this
swamp to the Thames and following what was very probably
the course taken ,by the Waikato river before it broke
through the Taupiri gorge.   Whether they get this line of
rail or not, the reclamation of the swamp, about to be
undertaken, it is said, will at all events allow the formation
of a road to the navigation of the Piako, and thus put
Waikato in direct communication with the Thames gold
fields.

Fourteen miles from Hamilton we reached Cambridge, the
furthest settlement up the Horotiu and situated at one of

the base angles of the Waikato triangle, Alexandra being the other, and Ngaruawahia the apex. There is a great likeness about every one of these frontier townships, and in Waikato they all present the very good sign of being small, a proof that the country is prospering and that the inhabitants of the district are living on their farms. The Horotiu runs pretty swiftly here, and, under a good bridge which spans it, whirls about over the boulders encumbering its bed which must prove a nuisance to the angler who finds that the two pounder he has on his fly will persist in trying to get under them, and thereby rubs the silk or the casting-line to the imminent danger of its breaking.

From Cambridge I started for Taupo; but, before quitting the Delta, a short retrospect may not be out of place. The reader has seen Waikato under two aspects, there is also an intermediate stage which deserves attention. The first European who ascended the Waipa River found its banks inhabited by a large and savage native population, whose sole delight and occupation was—warfare. It was with a view to preeminence in this that the people toiled laboriously and prepared by hand labour the flax which they bartered for guns and ammunition. Eternally at war with other tribes, or among themselves, the continuous series of fights which took place and the practice so prevalent of wholesale slaughter after a victory helped materially to thin their numbers to a considerable extent.

The next feature was the advent of the missionaries; and, under the influence of the new doctrines preached by them, and adopted by the natives with a surprising rapidity, peaceful habits were introduced, and agriculture succeeded to strife; large tracts of land were laid down in wheat, supplying to a great extent the Auckland market; mills were built; schools were erected; and for a time all was prosperity and peace. With every belief in the thorough conversion of

N

their pupils, the zealous propagators of the faith allowed
themselves to be carried away by their enthusiasm, and
fancied they had deeply implanted the seeds of religion, when
their disciples had adopted in reality only the outer
ceremonies prescribed to them; in many cases, such as the
observance of the Sunday as a day of rest, carrying their
notions of strictness even beyond those of their preceptors.
The attempt to eradicate from a full grown generation, and
at one swoop, all ancestral notions and to replace them
in its untutored mind by a religion which was entirely op-
posed to its former ideas, has been confessed to have been in
ninety-nine cases out of a hundred a failure. The old
leaven still lay there, and a proof of the truth of this came
once under my own observation. A tribe I knew very well
had been for years under missionary care; they had built a
church for their worship; had retained their Christian faith
whilst in arms against us; and, after submission, had once
more quietly settled down to their old agricultural pursuits,
living on terms of perfect harmony with the inhabitants of
the new settlement which had been formed in their midst.
The Hau Hau fanaticism arose on the West Coast, and
emissaries were sent round to the East, who succeeded in
some cases too well in their mission. In the instance of this
particular tribe, one morning the villages were found
deserted; men, women, and children had flung their old
faith to the winds at the instigation of a few Hau Hau
delegates, and had disappeared into the interior. Their leading chiefs were in Auckland, and this may account for the
ease with which the tribe was led away; but it was not till
these returned, and, accompanied by energetic officers of the
Government, hunted up the absentees, that they once more
changed their minds, and returned to their old homes. It
need scarcely be said that this exodus so unsettled their
minds, that their exact faith now would be a matter of

difficulty to ascertain with preciseness. Few in number in comparison with their flocks, it was of course impossible for the early missionaries to pay to the education of the children that attention which alone could lead to the civilization of the entire race. What they had not the means of doing, can be carried out by the Legislature, under whose auspices village schools are starting up in all directions; schools where instruction in the English language is a *sine quâ non*, and where every effort is made to train the youthful mind into the ways of European thought. Not that the desired result will be gained in the one generation; it is only with time that a complete revulsion can be made in the habits and reason of an entire race. Energetic as the missionaries were, they made mistakes; and gradually, as a body, they lost the influence they had at the outset acquired so rapidly.

It has been seen above (v. Page 57) how, some years ago, a feeling arose among the Maories that the contiguity of European farmers to native cultivators would be productive of dissensions as to trespass of cattle, &c.. There can be but little doubt that behind this pretext lay a fear of the ever-spreading wave of population which threatened to supplant them in their ancestral patrimonies, and a dread of losing irretrievably lands endeared to them by long possession and legendary traditions. Still there were to be found individuals ready to part with their property in exchange for the good things the pakeha brought; and it was this which made the natives combine in an anti-land-selling league, and endeavour to fix a boundary beyond which the white man was to own no property. To carry out this idea and their own views of reform and order among themselves, a King was elected: and in 1863, from a variety of causes, the Waikato tribes were in arms. The result is known: they have lost the land they so dearly prized. There has lately however been a change which has made itself apparent by a some-

what freer intercourse between the two races on the frontier.
The settlers, short of labour, have been but too glad to
employ their dusky neighbours; and these have not less will-
ingly taken pakeha wages.   The sick too, have found out that
they have only to come in to the settlements, and indeed in
cases to request the Government medical officer to visit them
at their villages, to experience the benefit of remedies unknown
to themselves.   There have been meetings between the
Friendlies and the Kingites, in which the former have
spoken their minds out pretty freely in favour of roads, &c.,
through the country, to the disappointment of the latter;
and generally there has been an increased degree of intercourse
which seems to pave the way for the abolition at some
future period of the self-imposed exile in which the Waikato have been living for past years.

NOTE.—Since the above chapter was written a fresh outrage has
taken place on the Waikato frontier; a European was murdered last
April by a party of natives who have sought and found shelter among
the King party.   The relative situations of the two races on the
frontier, the one occupying lands of which the other has been dis-
possessed, are in themselves favourable to the commission of
occasional acts of violence, and I see no reason to retract anything
I have said above, especially as all proceedings since the murder go
to prove the entire isolation of the King party from the great body
of friendly natives.

CHAPTER VI.

TAUPO.

From the Waikato to Taupo two different lines of road exist : one by the old mail track, disused since the war, running from Orakau by Aniwaniwa, where the Waikato rapids were crossed over a fallen tree ; the other, from Cambridge up the right bank of the river. It was the latter which I had to adopt, and even here there was a choice, as one track led a little more inland than the other ; the native who acted as my guide took me by the former, the least frequented and easy of the two. After leaving Cambridge the road passes a good distance through lands occupied as sheep runs : for some four or five miles it is fit for waggons ; and, turning off then to the left, it leads up to Matamata and the Ngatihaua settlement where stands the monument to William Thompson.* From this turn the track is only fit for horses and traverses country which, however agreeable it may be to the eyes of a settler on the look out for a run, possesses but little interest to the general traveller. There were slight ups and downs, valleys with small swamps, and fern hills with a sprinkling of bush about them ; but it was some little distance out of Cambridge before any spot was reached from which could be obtained anything like a view. It was just after getting out of a small belt of bush that the top of a saddle was attained, commanding enough to afford a really fair prospect. To the eastward lay an extensive valley

---

* Thompson was the leading spirit in the war of 1863, but had submitted before his death, on which event an English admirer of his character erected a monument to his memory.

through whose marshes meandered numerous streams flowing northward to unite together and form the Thames and Piako, whose waters empty themselves into the Hauraki Gulf; beyond it again, steep and rugged on our side, but on their further flank sloping gradually towards Tauranga, ran a chain of hills fissured by ravines and clad with the sombre hue so characteristic of New Zealand forests. Following with the eye the northward course of the range, a bold outstanding mass was pointed out as the Aroha* Mountain, that cynosure of Auckland speculators, within whose bosom are believed to exist incalculable riches in the shape of quartz reefs: right in rear lay the whole Delta of the Waikato rolled out like a panorama, its two confining rivers gleaming in the sunshine as each pursued its course; the sluggish Waipa in a series of sinuous bendings, twisting and turning through the limestone country it traverses; the swift Horotiu steadily keeping in almost a straight line the path it has pierced for itself through the soft sandy soil; the former the emblem of pliancy, the latter the personification of dogged strength. Through the glasses could be distinctly seen the houses in each settlement, looking like so many toy cottages; and, beyond them, Taupiri closed in, and no trace appeared of the pass by which the Waikato finds its outlet. To the right I could catch no glimpse of the river which here rolls at the foot of a consecutive series of terraces, three in number, if I remember rightly; at one place, Aniwaniwa, forcing its way through a rocky gorge, so narrow that a fallen tree spans it, and down which it roars and tumbles and foams with many a whirlpool and heavy swirl: but it flowed between us and the towering peaks of Mangatautari which rise in solitary grandeur from the plateau of Upper Waikato. Ahead were masses of peaks and wooded heights: and, still a sure guide to locality, could be perceived the snowy

---

* Aroha (love).

summits of the two giants who keep silent watch and ward
over the sterile deserts of Taupo. Far, far away to the
right I thought I could discern a faint white speck, which,
from its direction, should have been Mount Egmont, in
Taranaki, but of this there was no certainty. This was the
last glimpse of Waikato; and, after winding through a
glen or two, we reached a more sterile part where the fern
began to get scrubbier and scrubbier, and to give way occasionally to tussocky grass. There were inconvenient little
places too in the shape of swampy banked creeks which had
to be jumped, on one occasion my horse landing in a soft
place, sending me flying, and nearly rolling down on to his
back in the narrow stream. It was decidedly uninteresting
travelling, especially as deuce a track could I see, and my
guide's horse now got slower and slower in his pace, till a walk
was all that could be extracted from him. It was getting dusk;
still the brute could not be hurried; and darkness overtook
us in a small hollow, where my aboriginal friend declared
his inability to get further on. There ought to be a track
about, he said, but he was off it, and we must halt till daylight. Pleasant this; there was not a bit of wood for a fire,
nor a drop of water anywhere at hand; we had no "kai,"
and all there was for my horse to eat was the corn I had on
my saddle. However, there was no help for it; blundering
about in the dark would probably have resulted in horse
and man getting bogged; so, unsaddling, and tying the
tether rope to my arm (the only hold about to which it could
be fastened) I took a pull at the flask, wrapped myself up
in my 'possum with the saddle for a pillow (and when
properly managed this makes an uncommonly good one), and
lit my pipe. It was a glorious night, though coolish. The
stars were out by the million, or billion—numbers in such a
case don't much matter—and it was impossible to lie there,
looking upward to the countless glories of the sky without

falling into meditation. I can almost understand the prairie-fever which novelists talk of as seizing the traveller on the vast plains of the regions of the West; the precise feeling cannot be described, but, while going about and camping out, whether in bush or open, a strange sort of sensation of independence comes over one, as if one were rid of the cares and anxieties of the world. There is pleasure in such occasional solitude, with no companionship but that of the horse whose movements while grazing are the only sign of life around; in feeling that one is one's master for the nonce, and servant too; in watching the blue curls of the soothing tobacco; in speculating on what lies overhead; and finally, in turning round in the warm 'possum, and, despite the hard ground, sinking into the sleep well earned by the day's work. So much for the open plain bivouac; another phase of nature presents itself to the traveller comfortably ensconced in the bush between the roots of some huge tree, a good fire blazing at his feet. Here, all is gloom, save where a streak of moonlight wends its way through the thick foliage and lights up with a silvery sheen the ferns and mosses carpeting the ground; there is no longer the unbroken stillness and silence of the plains; for, while the lonely cry of the more-pork and the occasional rustle of a branch brushed by a passing night bird fall on the ear, strange sounds, mysterious creakings and groans, and occasionally a crash resounding far and wide and indicating the fall of some ancient tenant of the mountain sides, tend as much to murder sleep as silent contemplation of the star-lit sky. But it is chiefly when camping out in the open on nights like these that the profound problem of the rules which govern the orbs sparkling in illimitable space, nay, of one's very existence and destiny, forces itself prominently forward; and, if at any time, it is then that the mind realizes, as it were, the infinite and obtains a conception of the littleness of man, of his belongings, and of the theories which conceive the worlds above to have been created merely for his special use and delectation.

In order however, to be able to indulge properly in reveries of the above kind one thing is necessary. The night must be fine : for a wet jacket, sodden blankets, and a heavy downpour of rain play the very deuce with all romantic feelings, and induce no higher aspirations than vain wishes for warm beds and watertight ceilings.

The next morning the track was found, not two hundred yards off. How I blessed my native friend ! His horse being still pumped, I cantered on at dawn, and pulled up at Te Whetu, a Maori *kainga*, where the natives were evidently astonished to see me. I must explain that these were Ngatiraukawas, and that this ride was taken before their renunciation of allegiance to the King, mentioned in the last chapter. There was evidently some surprise at seeing a pakeha come up by himself, but at the same time there was abundant hospitality : my horse was taken from me, unsaddled, and led off to water and grass, and I was inducted into the "*whare-runanga*" while breakfast (and supper) was getting ready : this, by the way, consisted of a fresh killed pigeon, boiled without having been drawn ; and we were all as thick as thieves by the time my guide came up. One chap did glower at me for a long time, squatting with his blanket up to his mouth and staring as none but a Maori can stare, but at last he left off this amusement, and to my astonishment told me he knew me very well. I rather fancied that when we had last seen each other, it had not been on an occasion so pacific as the present. However, he was as jolly as the rest, and right welcome they made me. Contrasting strongly with the low dens in which the tribe nightly chokes off to sleep was a huge *whare* built for the accommodation of the delegates at a *runanga* (council) about

to be held.   The ridge pole was fully 20 feet from the floor,
and the centre post supporting it was carved to represent a
tribal ancestor : in length, the house was some forty feet,
and in breadth about twenty, the side walls up to the eaves
being lined with "toe-toe" stalks, stained in different patterns ;
the roofing and sides were of course of raupo, both projecting over the doorway, so as to form a porch, where the
indolent natives might bask quietly in the sunshine,
or sleep in that wonderfully uncomfortable attitude which
none but a Maori can adopt.   Most nations, even of
savages, like to have something under their heads in the
shape of a pillow; but this adjunct to comfort is not recognised by the Maori who coils himself up in his blanket
so that not an inch of him is visible, lies down on the bare
ground, and snores away happily.

Soon after leaving Te Whetu, with a fresh guide and
horse, we came upon the pumice plateau which I
had been led to expect, as bleak, dreary, an expanse as
it had yet been my lot to traverse ; there were hollows in it
similar to those read of as occurring in sandy deserts, and all so
wofully alike that, where no path existed, it was marvellous
how a way could be known.   We rode on a few miles till
a sudden turn introduced me to new scenery.   We were in
one of the above mentioned hollows, when Hemiona wheeled
off to the right between two hillocks of pumice sand ; I followed of course, and my astonishment can be conceived at
finding that these mounds merely concealed two huge
blocks of rock which seemed the portals to another world ;
for, straight below, lay a deep ravine, the way down to
it being by a cleft between two walls of precipitous rock.
The descent was not easy, even though we dismounted, for
there were a good many boulders and loose stones knocking
about, but we got safe to the bottom.   I could now realise
what I had read of "cañons" in books of American travel,

for this was one, and no mistake. Some 800 or a 1000 feet above our heads the plain was traversed by a chasm which sank sheer for about a quarter of the way down, the remaining part consisting of a steep slope formed by the *débris* of rock which had crumbled away in the course of ages; the width of the gulch from lip to lip I guessed at about 250 yards. Looking **up** the ravine, the further end was closed by dense bush, proving the length of time which must have elapsed since torrents wore out this huge drain, if torrents formed the erosive power; and, at its lower extremity, it opened into a basin from which branched out similar chasms. Following one of these, I found we had not yet reached the lowest level, for a descent of another fifty feet brought us to a limpid brook slowly wending its way to join the Waikato. We had crossed this, and I was wondering how on earth we were to get out of the gigantic trap we were in when Hemiona pointed to a zig-zag line along the side some distance ahead, where the slope appeared not quite so steep, and said that was our path. As above the talus there rose certainly a hundred feet of bare smooth rock, I guessed my friend was chaffing; but, not a bit of it: arrived at the foot he jumped off, gave his horse a lick, and the beast began scrambling up hill. Once the ascent commenced, I ceased to interest myself in the fate of my nag or companion, for all I looked after was my own personal safety, so abrupt was the rise and so slippery the scanty grass under the feet. It was not till close to the wall of rock that a narrow slit, that is the only word I have for it, was visible. It was just broad enough for the horses, and both they and their riders were not sorry to emerge again into the upper regions. From this we kept on through the same uninteresting kind of country, bordered on our left by the bush which extends from this away to Lake Rotorua, and we jogged on in silence till, pulling up literally

at the brink of a precipice, I beheld rolled out below a bit of
scenery which was to say the least, a marvellous sight.
Many hundred feet below extended a vast plain enclosed on all sides, and, but for the absence of fiery
lava streams, bringing to memory the description of
the volcano of Kilauea. Winding through it and making
its exit by some hidden rent far to the right ran the Waikato, while other streams could be traced pouring down
their tribute to swell the main river; a whitish line running
eastward was the road leading to Tauranga, and all around
the basin rose an encircling coronet of hills suggesting the
possibility of their having in ages past formed the cliffs of
a prehistoric lake. To the left at some few miles distance
shot up the rocky peaks of Paeroa, dark and grim looking,
and rendered more grim by a black thunder cloud against
which their jagged edges shewed in dim relief. The picture
was perfect; there was before me plain and river, mountain
and forest; and each under different aspects; for, while the
gloom of the approaching squall enhanced the weird and
desolate aspect of the precipices on the flanks of Paeroa,
the rays of the sun, now sinking in the west, peeping through
a break in the bank of clouds which lowered overhead, fell
on the surface of the river and threw a sheeny glare upon its
sinuous stream.

I have said the view was grand; I may add that after
gazing on it with pleasure for some time, I lost some sense
of its beauties on learning that once more we were off the
track; the real truth being that since the climb out of the
deep ravine there had been no track at all, and that we had
not touched the right one since leaving Te Whetu. We
looked to the right, we looked carefully to the left; nowhere
did a sign exist of a break; and a chamois with frosted hoofs
could not have kept his feet on the slope below us.
Hemiona insisted upon it that our way lay to the right; and

as I could not contradict him, I followed his guidance. It took a good hour's ride along the brink of the cliffs before we came upon a spur which could be pronounced safe. So once more jumping off, down we went, sometimes sliding on short grass, sometimes sinking over the ankles in loose pumice till we reached the bottom. From this to Niho-o-te-kiore (*the Rat's tooth*), a kainga on the Waikato, was but a six or seven miles ride during which we passed the first solfataras we had seen on the way. A canoe took us across the river, and, thoroughly tired out, I was not long in disposing of dinner and tot, and in turning into bed. I thought I knew pretty well what strange sleeping places were, but here I was introduced to a novelty. The hut was built against a pumice cliff, into which the inmates were cutting a chimney, the resulting pumice sand being heaped up in the *whare*. For my accommodation this was nicely hollowed out in the centre ; a lot of raupo was laid on it covered by a mat, and over all came my 'possum. I don't know whether it was that I was tired, or what; but certainly I felt perfectly luxurious lying down on my sandy couch, and surrounded by a lot of inquisitive new friends of the native race, some of whom evidently were practised in European habits, for they insisted on "shouting" rum, and that highly doctored, for all hands.

From Niho-o-te-kiore to Tapuacharuru, on the shores of Lake Taupo, the road has been formed by native labour, the engineering portion of course being European, and reflects a good deal of credit on designer and workmen. The Waikato is to be bridged at Niho,* and, once a road established between Cambridge and this spot, the communication will be open from Auckland to Wellington. The importance of even this part of it will be best understood when it is known that it passes close to the spot where poor Lieut.

---

* This bridge is completed now.

Meade narrowly escaped with his life in 1865, an episode capitally described in his work. The narrative of his ride in the interior is indeed right throughout most graphic; there is not one word of exaggeration to be found in it, and it is quite refreshing to come across a work the author of which has to describe marvels of nature, and describes them enthusiastically, and yet truthfully. Now, instead of a narrow track as he found it, about which lurked ambushed savages, there was a broad highway along which I cantered in comfort for about twelve miles, sometimes winding through a ravine by sidings cut high above the stream, sometimes pushing on straight over flats, once native cultivations; and constantly catching glimpses of white curling vapour, indicating the presence of hot springs.

The lake itself is not seen till the traveller is close to its cliffs, and the river must be crossed before a fair view can be obtained of its dimensions. The point at which Taupo is struck is called Tapuacharuru (sounding-footsteps), a capital name, as anyone will testify who has listened to the hollow reverberation of his horse's hoofs while cantering over the ground. · A cliff juts out here into the lake, crowned by a palisaded pa now tumbling to pieces, in which I once ran a chance of standing a siege; and just at its foot, after traversing the whole lake and depositing in its transit any impurities gathered in its course from the foot of Ruapehu, the Waikato River rolls out in a broad and deep current, whose clearness, transparency, and colour remind the tourist of the Rhone at Geneva. The river crossed in a canoe, a view of the lake is obtained from the bank on which stands the Constabulary redoubt. It takes some time to appreciate Taupo, especially if the tourist has in mind the engraving in Hochstetter's book; one cannot at first look at the lake, at its shores low to the south, high and wood-crowned to the north, for involuntarily the eye turns towards the two snowy peaks which dwarf every hill around. Those plateaux to the south-west terminating in the sheer cliffs of Karangahape, rising fully a thousand feet out of the waters at their base, the bush covered heights, broken into many a bay, which border the northern extremity, the cones jutting up beyond Tokanu—baby volcanoes as it were—all look so small by the side of Tongariro and Ruapehu that they lose any grandeur they might possess if no overshadowing majesty were near. **Then the** southern shore **is tame, and it is** useless to try and find **out** the beauties of **that** opposite it, for to whatever point the eye is turned, **it is** bound to come round to the main attraction, **those** two **white** summits shooting up towards the clouds. Habit does **a** great deal; and after many attempts, one can **arrive at a** pitch of mental concentration, and steadily consider the lake, and nothing more. Even then Taupo Moana—for dignified it is by the name of a sea—is not lovely; there is nothing soft about it; neither is there at a glance to be caught anything grand. Devoid of the ruggedness of Highland lochs, it yet possesses none **of the** smiling beauties which render so charming the Italian lakes; **it is a** sombre piece of water **which,** situated in the midst **of sterility,** harmonises **well with its surroundings.**

But though **unlovely in itself it yet** possesses grand accompaniments. **Away beyond the** south-west extremity, with many a lower peak **around,** from the bosom of a vast forest rise the two great mountains, Tongariro **and** Ruapehu, the latter a huge unshapely mass, the former an elegant cone; on the summit of each lies eternal snow, but a bare rocky spot on Tongariro whence issues a jet of steam, dwarfed to insignificance by the distance, still shews the existence of internal fires which occasionally reveal their presence by rumblings and thunderings loud enough to be

heard as far as Tauranga.   Southward, some thirty miles
from the lake, stretches the chain of the Kaimanawa, touching to the east the Uriwera mountains, on the west sloping
down into the Patea plateau and forming a long barrier
through which exist but few passes.   Westward, a chaotic
assemblage of mountains indicates the regions of the Tuhua,
and nearer at hand, to the east, a solitary hill, Tauhara,
starts out of the plain, its shape asserting its volcanic origin.
For the rest, east and south for miles stretches a barren
plateau.   Such is the picture presented from Tapuacharuru.
Taupo Moana, 1200 feet above the sea, is a spot celebrated
in native history.   Here it was that dwelt a cruel *taniwha*,
who even now makes his presence known by the constant agitation of the water between Motukaiho, the only
island, and the main land; it was here that Mount
Egmont had his disagreement with his brother Tongariro;
numerous legends exist to account for the volcanic communications between it and the burning mountain of White
Island,—and generally speaking it was looked upon as the
"omphalos" of "Te ika a Maui."   Near its banks it was that
one of the old school of chiefs, Te Heuheu, reported to
have been a giant in size, was with many of his tribe, over-
whelmed in a land slip; of him a story is related that,
being rather harassed by missionaries of different persuasions,
he made answer somewhat to the following effect: "You
tell me to worship in your fashion; another pakeha comes
and says if I don't go his way I shall suffer; and a third
arrives to contradict you both.   Which of you is right?   I
can't decide; but I think my way quite as good as any you
propose, and to that I shall stick."

   For some time it was supposed Taupo was fathomless; it
has however been sounded by an officer on the spot, and at
no very great depth; so there is one bit of tradition knocked
on the head by a practical experiment.   In its native waters

no native fish are to be found, but some carp introduced seem to be thriving well, as a few specimens in good condition were caught in Maori nets a good way from where they had been put in. To the credit of the natives be it said that, knowing the value the pakeha set on the few fish brought up so far at some expense, they at once turned out again those they had hauled up.

I believe Taupo has the credit of being an ancient crater. There are numerous other indications of plutonic agency: the soil for miles is many feet deep in pumice sand originally ejected from the bowels of the earth; and so it is reasonable to suppose that at some time or other, there was some pretty hot work hereabouts, the sole remaining evidences of which are the rare and mild outbursts of Tongariro, and the numberless solfataras scattered around. Except on the flanks of the twin mountains there is but little trace of lava, and it is a moot point whether the pumice sand forming the plains is not a subaqueous formation. There is evidence in favour of this theory; for, in the sidings which have been cut to form the Napier road, trunks of trees have been found in a horizontal position. One I saw was that of a large fern tree converted completely into charcoal; it was some fifteen feet in length, and was covered by about ten or twelve feet of pumice; how much of the same soil lay under it could not of course be guessed.

At Tapuaeharuru, I missed on this occasion seeing my genial and stout friend, Poihipi Tukairangi, who behaved very kindly to Meade during his tour, and who, with his hapu, a section of the Arawa, stuck manfully to our side while war was raging around him. The first thing after arrival, and due telegraphy, was of course a swim, and then arrangements as to the morrow's doings.

After breakfast we started off on horseback, a party of four or five bound for the "Huka" waterfall; it was a lovely

morning, and hot enough in all conscience, so we took it
easy and jogged along quietly in single file, carefully following the track.   This is a precaution not to be neglected; for
here and there on either hand, a slight depression over
which hovers a thin mist-like steam denotes rotten ground
with underlying heat which would play the very mischief
with man or beast who had the ill-luck to roll into it.   The
hollow sound elicited by the hoofs of the horses when put to
a quiet trot brought up classical ideas, and actually elicited
a quotation as a proof that Virgil knew what it was to
canter over a volcanic country.   The line—

    Quadrupetante sonu putrem petit ungula campum

does give a sort of idea of the queer reverberation under foot.
But Latin at Taupo! with a Maori chief at one's side! and
quoted by an Armed Constable too!   *Quousque tandem!*
After about a couple of miles ride we struck the river where
it makes a sharp bend between two high cliffs, those on our
side receding from the brink and forming a small amphi-
theatre around a diminutive flat.   The steep left bank was
covered with luxuriant ferns, but that on the right looked
exactly what it was, bare, burnt, crumbling earth, presenting
the most desolate aspect: one could almost imagine it to be
a fire-ruin.   Scrambling down a slope, not much affected by
the internal heat, we reached the river's edge, and halted
opposite a queer looking funnel-like cone sticking a few feet
out of the ground, apparently composed of sticks cemented
together by a sinter deposit similar to that formed at Rotomahana.   It is hardly fair to tell tales out of school, so I
must abstain from mentioning the practical joke usually
played here upon the unsuspicious stranger : the proper thing
to do is to administer pills in the shape of small sods thrown
down the funnel ; presently there is heard a grunting, gurg-
ling sound, and out comes the bolus flying high into the
air followed by the propelling power, a column of hot water,

Another mile's ride brought us to a stream and small cascade of water rather too hot to be pleasant, and here we left our horses and took a *waka*. This was decidedly pleasant travelling; there was scarcely any necessity for using the paddles, so evenly **and quietly we** glided with the current on the bosom of the stream; **hot was** no name for it, and with coats off and handkerchiefs supplementing the puggerees we reclined at length, allowing the two most energetic of the party to carry on a pretence **of paddling.** The banks as we passed them presented a perfect **contrast: that on the** right, rising gradually towards **low** hills, was clad with verdure, though that was only fern, tutu, and koromiko or cabbage trees, with here and there a patch of cultivation surrounding a Maori *whare* or two; a few creeks bordered by stumpy peach trees opened out to the river, and in them the aboriginal population, male and female, was diving about in great glee. The other side was different: a narrow strip separated the river from a steep but not high rise forming a plateau cleft at intervals by a series of ravines **running** inland, and the whole was covered with **low parched** scrub fern. Slowly and lazily we drifted **down till a** murmur gradually increasing in intensity **warned us of** the proximity of rapids; **but** just as our **pace** was **becoming** faster, a sweep of the **paddle** turned the nose of **the** *waka* into a little creek, **and we jumped ashore.** Following the river we passed the rapids **above** mentioned, **and,** rising a short ascent, became conscious that an uncertain noise lately distinguishable was now a full-mouthed roar coming from ahead: another bit of climb, and the Huka* was in view. At this particular spot the river is about a hundred and fifty yards wide, and right across it runs a massive reef some hundred and twenty yards in thickness; it can be easily conceived that at some

---

* Huka (froth or foam; snow.)

period or another the whole river was carried bodily over
this dyke, but that some convulsion of nature during the
volcanic disturbances by which this region has been so
wonderfully tossed about gave it a new way of escape.
About the centre of the barrier, extending in a direct line
straight through the thickness of the reef, yawns a chasm
only fifteen yards in width, into whose open jaws the river
hurls itself with tremendous velocity.   We walked on
further, till we stood on the actual rock, and peered over the
brink at the torrent boiling but a few feet below us.   A half
moon shaped rapid some hundred yards above the reef pre-
pares the river for its race and sends it right up to the
mouth of the rift where it takes its first downward shoot in
one smooth oily green wave which, actually, a little further
on, dives into and under a tormented and seething mass of
white water; then follows another tolerably clear shoot,
charging, as it were, another confused mass of foam; then
another dive, and more bubbling and tossing which lasts
until the reef sinks sheer down, and the river takes a leap
of forty or fifty feet into a glorious pool surrounded by cliffs.
We stood for some time watching the curious way in which
the smooth shoots seemed to slide into and under the foam
caused by obstructive rocks, speculating as to the pace
attained, and amusing ourselves by throwing in sods and
sticks: odd enough, at one particular spot, the lightest
thing which has hitherto floated on the surface takes a
sudden header, and is no more seen.   Whether this is caused,
as stated, by the convex shape the surface of the water takes
in consequence of the enormous pressure on the side walls,
or not, I cannot tell; but down went every bit of wood we
chucked in.   Some twenty yards down from the entrance of
the chasm, on the right bank jutted out a small ledge of
rock, hardly broad enough for a man to stand on, but supporting a tree whose roots had somehow or another found

nourishment in cracks and crevices;—and this ledge plays
an important part in the tradition handed down concerning
the Huka. We got to the end of the reef, and walking
round the horse-shoe cliff till we obtained a full view of the
cataract, we lay down on the short grass, lit pipes, and
listened to the tale imparted by the old native who had accompanied us. This is what he related :—

"Eight or more generations ago," he said, "one of our
Taupo people went down to Wanganui and there happened
to meet a chief much given to bragging. This chief came to
him and questioned him about the Huka. This chief
laughed at the idea of its being impassable. He said—" I
have many falls and rapids in my country, and I have eaten
(shot) them all. It is you who are afraid : I will come
and show you how to eat the Huka." He came accordingly
with seventy men, and they obtained a large canoe for the
purpose of making the experiment; on the day when they
were going to try it, they took with them the Taupo native
who had told them about the place. Many people assembled
to see this Wanganui chief conquer the Atua of the Huka ;
but they did not believe it could be done. Some were on
one side of the chasm ; some on the other ; and some sat
just here to see the canoe come down the fall. They started ;
they got well over the first small rapid; the canoe entered
the first wave and shot down rapidly. The rowers were
elated with the prospect of success, and to a man they stood
up in the canoe and shouted in triumph. But the Taupo
man felt afraid ; he was in the bow ; and just as they neared
the white water, he took a great spring, landed on the small
bit of rock which sticks out there and clung to the tree ; from
that he was easily pulled up. But the canoe got into the
foam ; it hit the rock, it broke, and all the crew were in the
water; they were swept down ; and just where you saw sink
the pieces of wood you threw in, they all disappeared ! Some

of the bodies were afterwards found well down the river;
and to this day, when the water is very low, we can perceive
occasionally the nose of the canoe which is jammed between
some rocks just at the fall. Often we see its "*Atua*" (Spirit):
there—there;—you can see it now—that colour on the
spray!" It would have been of no use enlightening the
old gentleman as to the meaning of an Iris, so we did not
disturb his belief, but just lay there smoking, basking in
the heat and enjoying a regular *dolce far niente*.

We rode back by a different track, meaning to have a
warm bath at a spot a little distance off where a hot spring
issues from a marsh in a bubbling stream, and runs down
through a narrow gully; but on dismounting and looking at
the waters it was voted unanimously that on such a roasting
day as this a plunge in the cold lake would be far more
seasonable, and so we went on. An attempt is being made
in this ravine to make the hot water baths comfortable, by
diverting the stream into pools which are to be surrounded
by dressing places, &c., the originator of this Taupo spec
being, I believe, *the* Taupo guide, Jack Loffley, whom I can
conscientiously recommend to any tourist, never having
employed him myself in that capacity, but having seen
him in one or two ticklish moments of the kind which test
what sort of stuff a man is made of. A stranger at first
sight would perhaps be startled at his attire, but after all it
is, minus the arms, &c., the very same garb nine-tenths of
the Colonial Forces, officers and men, used to adopt on
service, consisting of a flannel shirt, sleeves rolled up, a
shawl worn kilt fashion, shoes and long stockings: to this
dandies added a blue serge jumper. Such a dress is at first
rather uncomfortable for the knees when going through a
bush full of "lawyers;" or, a trifle worse if possible, through
high burned fern, with the charred stalks, now sharp pointed,
preserving the inclination acquired, when green, under the

influence of constant winds, and bent down in opposition
to one's progress. But then in river work its advantages are
palpable : you have to cross a river—say sixty times in one
day's march, and that is not an out-of-the-way number ; the
trouser-wearing warrior finds a baggy weight gradually increasing about his ankles as sand imperceptibly invades his
nether garments, well tucked in to his socks as they are ;
there is a drag about the waist, and perpetual are the
" hitchings-up" and halts to wring out the part flopping about
his ankles : not so with him of the kilt ; on entering a stream
he simply lifts up his garment, wades through, and ten
minutes afterwards is as dry as ever. Notwithstanding
this rather savage costume and his slightly brimstony
nickname, no tourist will repent having put himself in
Loffley's hands.

One place which I was very sorry not to be able to visit,
Orakei-korako, an old ferry on the Waikato, is celebrated for
the number and activity of its geysers, and for alum caves
which contain huge stalactites. A trip to this and to Tokanu, on the Western shores of the lake, together with a
climb up Tongariro, form part of a programme which I have
not yet been able to carry out. It struck me more than
once during the journey that it would be possible to canoe
from Onehunga to Wanganui. Crossing the Manakau from
the former place, Waikato Heads can be reached by the
Awaroa near Waiuku, and thence, with but a few portages,
the canoeist can easily get to Taupo, cross the lake and
enter the head waters of the Waikato : here would lie the
difficulty, that of transporting the canoe on to the Wanganui river, and I do not know enough of the country to
hazard a guess as to the feasibility of the task : but once upon
this stream, and a very romantic and beautiful one from all
accounts, there would be no difficulty, care being taken at the
numerous rapids, which however are constantly shot by the

natives in their *wakas*. I throw out the hint to any adventurous Rob-Royist in Auckland.

Taupo and Rotomahana, the latter for choice, must eventually become sanatoria in cases of cutaneous disease or of rheumatism. I have heard of some extraordinary cures under the first head; and, at my last visit to Taupo, I met a gentleman who, from rheumatism, had barely been able to get so far as Tapuaeharuru, but who now, after six weeks' bathing, was walking about as sound and upright as possible. He even had a swim with us in the lake.

Already there is coach communication between Taupo and Napier; it will not be long before Cobb and Co., run from Tauranga and Rotorua and thence join the main line; and it only needs the construction of a road over the country I had just passed—but in another direction, more to the westward, which would avoid the deep ravines I had to cross—to bring Auckland into direct coach traffic with Wellington; and then invalids will experience but little difficulty in reaching the spot.*

The road to Napier from Tapuaeharuru passes close to the foot of Tauhara and runs through Opepe, a constabulary station established at a junction of native tracks by which communication was formerly kept up between the East Coast rebels and the King party. It is a lonely spot, with however the advantage of a belt of timber close at hand, and of soil which will grow garden produce; a stout stockade renders the post safe against any attack, and the buildings, all constructed by the men, are very comfortable. But Opepe is a place of bitter memories to me, and never can I visit it without the most painful reminiscences of the tragic fate of the party of cavalry volunteers, who, on one

---

* Since writing the above, a bridge has been erected over the Waikato River at Niho-o-te-kiore, and the coach does run from Tauranga to Taupo.

occasion escorted me to Taupo.   It was almost impossible to
realize that this spot, now full of life and bustle, was the
same at which I arrived one morning at grey dawn from
Tapuaeharuru to find my poor fellows, among them two personal friends, lying stark and stiff.   Surprised by a force
more than ten times their number, it is a wonder any
escaped ; and that they were surprised is not a matter of
astonishment to any one who has ridden over these plains,
cut up as they are by ravines and gullies, in which a large
body of men could march with ease without being perceived by any one on the plateau itself.

From Opepe all is flat and bare till the ranges are
reached and only one river is met, the Rangitaiki, which,
leaving the Taupo plateau, flows eastward through the
Kaingaroa plains, as sterile and desert as those it has
quitted, washes the foot of the mountains forming the
northern boundary of the Uriwera, near Mount Edgcumbe
pours through a narrow defile, and lower down unites its
waters to those of the Tarawera river, both falling into the
sea at Matata, under the name of Te Awa o te Atua (the
river of the Spirit).

The herbage on these plains is confined to a short tussocky
grass, resembling slightly the toë-toë, inasmuch as the edges
of the leaves present, though to a slight degree, the same
serrated appearance.   The roots go but a little way down,
and I often used in former days to watch my poor horse pick
up bunch after bunch, not lovingly with his teeth, but
just with his lips ; the whole thing would come out of the
ground, and a slight munch or two was quite enough to
satisfy the unfortunate beast that it was the same vile stuff
he had tried so often before to satisfy his hunger ; so he would
lazily open his mouth, let go the tussock, and wander dis-
consolately till a greener looking bit deceived him again.
Had it not been for a few patches of koromiko found in the

Q

vicinity of the camp at Fort Galatea, every horse would
have died of starvation. As it was, they were all within an
inch of it. Away to the westward there is a difference.
The slopes of the Kaimanawa towards that point of the
compass are composed of fair soil; they are already taken
up as sheep runs, and there is a prospect of a further development of that part of the country by the formation of a road
between it and Wanganui.

Entering the defile through which rushes the Waipunga,
we come once more upon sidings and cuttings in
pumice sand cliffs, and, from the entry of the gorge,
the road becomes picturesque. It is carried high up
over the bed of the river on sidings whence can be
seen far below both cascades and rapids; then it
drops again to the level of the torrent, only to rise once
more on the opposite side; it winds along, heading the small
ravines and gullies which sink into the sides of the mountains, now passing through bits of level with thick bush on
either hand, now affording peeps into valleys and glens
whence comes the murmur of many waters; and again
it rises upwards by a series of zig-zags cut into the flanks of
steep fern-covered mountains.

Three posts of Constabulary occupy the line between the
plains and the Mohaka river. Runanga, on a hill 2000 feet
above the sea; Tarawera, almost on the bank of the river,
and Te Haroto, on the top of Turangakumu, about the same
altitude as Runanga. From this latter station one can
obtain a good idea of the general character around. In front
lies the valley of the Mohaka, a river which has cut a deep
channel for itself through what appears from our stand point
to be an unbroken plateau; beyond it, a white streak
running in and out along the side of the mountain facing us
denotes the road over Titiokura, and to the right and left
series after series of hills and mountains are jumbled up and

tossed about in the most confused manner. There seems to be some order in the ranges leading down to the sea, which are probably spurs running out from a central mass, but that centre portion, to all outward appearances, is utterly devoid of any regularity. On the summit of Turangakumu crops out a mass of dark conglomerate, thickly encrusted with fossil shells, and tough enough to make good road metal. In crossing these spurs to the eastward, on my way from Wairoa to Napier I found the same kind of formation very abundant, but much whiter, and apparently not so compact.

The Mohaka is a nasty river to cross; it is swift, freshes very rapidly, is very clear—so clear as to be eminently deceptive with regard to its depth, and runs over small slippery boulders. At my first attempt at it, looking down from the bank, I made sure the water would not be higher than my horse's knees; by the time I found it up to my saddle bow and forming quite a small wave at the wither I made a mental resolve in future always to use the ferry boat, and right glad I was to find myself clambering the narrow track which then led up the face of the steep cliff. Now a capital road has been constructed by cutting well down on the siding, and making a wide " return."

After this came a weary pull up Titiokura, but from the top of it there was a magnificent view of sea and land. Hawke's Bay was before me ; Scinde Island, the peninsula on which Napier is situated, looking like a solitary rock well out to sea, while beyond it Cape Kidnappers jutted out into the ocean, and hill rising after hill in the distance closed in the scene. From this the road dips into the valley of the Esk river ; and, after crossing and recrossing it till the mind is perfectly weary of counting the number of times, the traveller comes out on the shingle beach of Petane, a few miles from the Iron Pot, the harbour of Napier.

CHAPTER VII.

THE BAY OF PLENTY.

There are two ways of reaching Tauranga from Auckland, by sea, and overland. The road starts from the Thames gold-fields, passes through the unopened and tantalising Ohine-muri country, by the Kati Kati entrance to the inland waters of Tauranga harbour, and runs along their western shore till it strikes the township of Te Papa. A seventeen hours' passage in a steamer is however the easiest method of doing the journey, and the scenery exhibited by the Coast line is very picturesque, for, Cape Colville once rounded, the vessel sails along parallel to a line of high broken cliffs above which towers the Castle Rock of Coromandel; thickly clothed with bush, indented by numerous small inlets, sites of saw-mills, and here and there meeting the waves in a precipitous wall of rock, these hills, with their bold and rugged features, present a striking appearance. The inshore course, adopted by the small coasters, leads past a succession of islands scattered about in all directions, and of all sizes, from those containing hundreds of acres, to mere needles and pinnacles of rock. One small group, the Shoe and Slipper, I happen to know more of than I ever cared to learn; for, having for my sins taken a passage in a small schooner whose running rigging was commonly supposed to be composed of worn-out tether ropes, we got caught in a heavy gale; the skipper was very drunk, and would have run us stem on to a rock had he not been forcibly removed from deck in time, and we just managed to get under the

lee of the Slipper when our sails came tumbling down about
our ears. We had no boat, and all there was to eat on
board was a leg of mutton my servant had brought, but
there was no fuel to cook it with. However, another craft,
rather better found, was blown into the same shelter, and
I soon transhipped myself. But for three days we were
jammed here with nothing to do. Perhaps it was wrong,
but on a later occasion I could not help a feeling of satisfaction at seeing the bones of the " Hira," at last a total
wreck, deeply imbedded in the sand at the mouth of the
Opotiki River.

The entrance to Tauranga harbour lies between a sandy
strip of land and Mount Maunganui, which, from its height
of some 800 feet, acts as a landmark for miles. Rising
sheer out of the sea, and connected with the mainland by a
narrow belt of sand-hills, it resembles a Gibraltar in miniature, and history informs us that it once submitted to the
same fate as its prototype, having been taken by a surprise
and a *coup de main* on a stormy night. The seaward face
of the rock, exposed to the long sweep of the Pacific, is
hollowed out into little "combs" diminutively suggestive of
Devonshire coast scenes, and containing tons upon tons of
broken shells of the one kind, the volutes of a small conch.

On entering the harbour the view is really fine ; to the
right an estuary extends for sixteen miles till it communicates once more with the sea at the Kati Kati inlet ; to the
left rises the mountain, from its isolation appearing much
higher than it really is ; in front, a cluster of trees on a
promontory denotes the cemetery and mission station ; and,
from this, a plateau slopes gradually upwards till the horizon
is closed by a belt of bush some fourteen miles off. Inland
from the estuary, and to our right, the back country is
more broken, losing abruptly its character of an easy slope
and shooting up in peaks of a respectable altitude. Longing

eyes have often been turned in that direction, for in it lies the mountain range of the Aroha, believed to be a continuation of the auriferous chain of the Thames; and, beyond Kati Kati, are the Ohinemuri plains, whose richness in gold is all the more credited that the native owners persistently refuse to let the pakeha work on them.

There is not much to be seen at Tauranga: the township is only in its infancy, and the objects of local interest are chiefly confined to places remarkable in connection with the late war. Of course we went to see the Gate Pa, or what remains of it, where our troops got so thoroughly "whipped"; then we went on to Te Rangi, where they made up for their late defeat, and walked into the entrenchments with the bayonet; and from that we rode on to the edge of the bush whose shade was most grateful to men and horses. The country passed over was the gradually rising plateau I have mentioned, throughout bare of timber; great fissures traversed it, probably worn by water in days of old, but now dry ravines or swamps; the soil was of fair quality, but the absence of water and timber had evidently been one of the great preventions to its occupation. Tauranga was one of the military settlements; and, like most of the others, turned out a failure—so far as the original intention was concerned.

Lying lazily on the clover covered ground, and well shaded by a big "rimu," we had a perfect panorama before us. Tauranga harbour and the coast line, northward and southward for many miles could be all taken in at almost one glance; and out at sea rose several islands: the Great Barrier, a mountainous mass; Motiti, or Flat Island; and, nearest of all, Karewa, a rocky islet abounding in obsidian, and the home of a peculiar lizard, something like a small iguana. They are not handsome beasts these lizards, but they are pretty tenacious of life. One was sent a long distance by post, and arrived safe at his journey's end; another, I was assured, had eaten nothing for three weeks, and I was invited to go and look at it; in this case however, the fast had proved too protracted, and, when the box was opened, the brute was as dead as Julius Cæsar.

It was very pleasant **to loll** about out of the hot glare of the sun with nothing to do but watch **the pretty little** fan-tails swooping and diving all around us, their silvery under feathers glistening in the rays as they performed their fantastic antics close to our heads; and it was difficult to realize that some charred rails close by, and a stump which looked as if it had once belonged to a flag-staff, were the remains of a village, and of a pole around which I had, a few years before, by accident seen the Hau-Hau fanatics go through their worship and dance. A yacht had come into harbour, and its passengers were eager to see something of the interior of the country; so a few of us set all orders at defiance and rode up with them to this village. When first we sighted the place, the natives were engaged in their devotions, which consisted in going round and round the " niu," (or sacred pole), and grunting out exclamations, meaningless most of them, till they attained the *porewarewa* state of mental intoxication, in which condition the Hau-Haus conceived themselves inspired with the gift of tongues and jabbered away in Irish, French, German, &c., all of course perfect gibberish. **They** stopped as **we rode** up, and I must say that, though we very coolly dismounted, sat down, and made ourselves at home, we were not annoyed or molested in any way, but there was no doubt we were evidently considered " de trop." However, I don't think any of us felt sorry when on returning we had got clear of a nasty, ambushy-looking ravine, and stood once more on Pye's pa hill.

After all, they were not a bad lot these people of Orope (Europe, the name of the kainga), though they were Hau-

Haus. On one occasion they had in their hands one of our officers, who had been in the habit of wandering from his post after pigeons, never "fashing" himself about the natives. This time however, news had come about fighting somewhere down the coast ; Hakaraia, a chief of evil notoriety, was expected up ; so they kept my friend, and it was only after a deal of expostulation that he was allowed away : but even then some people had to go with him to prevent his falling in with any of the mob supposed to be on their way. He had not been long back in the block house at Pye's Pa, before Hakaraia did arrive with a lot of scoundrels, who would have thought it a good deed to tomahawk any pakeha, let alone an *apiha* (officer.)

Up to Orope we had been riding on a good made road, with bridges, culverts, &c., but behind us the bush was still thick and untouched. By this time it has assumed another aspect : a road has been cut through it ; the difficulties of the Mangarewa ravines are overcome ; the horseman who has breakfasted at Te Papa may take his evening swim in the warm waters of Lake Rotorua ; and mail coaches roll through a belt of bush, traversed till lately by a mere native track difficult even for pedestrians. In addition to improving the communication with the interior this road also opens up some country along the edge of the bush, and in it, where settlements are certain to arise as the land is of an excellent character.

During our stay at Tauranga we had an opportunity, while on a shooting excursion towards Kati Kati, of seeing some more country. Between the foot of the high range and the estuary lies a gentle slope of ground, intersected by numerous small streams and giving proof of its fertility by the heavy growth of "tupakihi," and tall fern which covers it ; this forms part of what was once confiscated territory. After the surrender of the Ngaiterangi tribe consequent on their complete defeat at Te Rangi, the Governor, Sir George Grey, in consideration of the honourable manner in which they had fought, returned to them three-fourths of their confiscated lands. This portion, with some exceptions for reserves, &c., was then purchased from them by the Government, and now presents eligible sites for settlements.

The Tauranga people are well aware of the value of these lands, and are not likely to rest satisfied till the road through them to the Thames, now in progress, is completed. Not only will this allow the Bay of Plenty settlers to send their stock to market and avoid risks of shipment, but the population of the district is likely to be increased by the close proximity to what is confidently asserted will be a payable goldfield. The moment the miner is allowed to peg out his claim on the spurs of the Aroha, or even at Ohinemuri, the prospects of Tauranga farmers are certain to improve.

Of course we visited the cemetery where lie the remains of the officers and men slain at the Gate Pa, at Te Rangi, and at the numerous skirmishes which have taken place in the vicinity between the colonial troops and the natives. Washed at its foot by the tide, and weakened by land springs, the whole point of land was gradually wearing away till actually some of the graves had crumbled down, and there was danger to the entire cemetery. A sea wall, constructed partly by the Navy and partly by the colonial forces, has arrested the decay. The other side of the tongue of land on which is situated the grave-yard shelves down to the "Judea" creek, at the ford of which one of H.M.'s Brigadier Generals was once wofully taken in by a couple of larking ex-diggers. The troops were crossing, when the General observed two men of the colonial forces busily engaged in "washing" some sand in their pannikins. For curiosity's sake, he asked what they were about, and with great

mystery the secret was revealed : there was some gold dust
at the bottom of the pannikins. The General took the
men's names, went on with the march, fully persuaded an
important discovery had been made, and on returning sent
for the two diggers. Of course they could not be found,
and the General learned at a very cheap rate how a mine
can be "salted," even in a bed of sand, by the judicious
introduction of the precious metal obtained elsewhere.

The shore opposite Tauranga is occupied by several
native villages, at one of which is established a very good
native school ; the largest kainga is Matapihi, where reside
the remnants of the Ngaiterangi tribe ; higher up is Hairini
(Cyrene) ; then on the inland waters we find Canaan and
Judea ; so there is plenty of proof that missionaries were
about when these names were given.

At Otumaetai, about two miles from the Judea ford,
used to be a Roman Catholic Church very prettily built in
the Maori *whare* style, with the interior lining of stalks of
the "toë-toë" (Prince of Wales feather grass), beautifully
stained and arranged in all manner of patterns ; it has
now however fallen altogether into disrepair.

Pretty scenery is to be found by boating up the Wairoa
river as far as a series of falls which it makes shortly after issuing from the bush ; or in dodging about among the numerous
small streams which fall into the harbour. Sites of old
pas, whether erected for intertribal warfare or defence
against our troops are frequent : near one of the latter,
at Te Puna, General Cameron had a narrow escape of being
captured with his staff, for a nice little ambuscade was laid
at the very spot where he meant to land from the steamer
to reconnoitre : luckily for him, he changed his mind, and did
not disembark.

As a military engineer it is well known that the Maori
has a natural talent ; and he readily adapts his defence to

the weapons brought against him. At the Gate Pa, the native flagstaff was erected well in rear of the entrenchments, of course misleading our gunners, who naturally concluded it must be in the centre of the place, and blazed away at it vigorously. I remember one proof of the readiness with which natives provide against any novelties in danger. Riding with several others in company with the chief Penetaka (the engineer of the Gate Pa), just after his first submission and before his second outbreak, we came upon a line of entrenchments barring the road. They were strong and well constructed, and not a soul of us (officers all) had been aware of their existence. Penetaka was questioned. —"Oh! yes," he said "these are the lines we built after the Gate Pa; then, after our defeat at Te Rangi, I had a quarrel here; Hakaraia insisted upon our taking up this position, but I objected. Now, if you were coming to attack this, what would you do?" The answer was obvious: there was an accessible mound at some distance on the flank from which the defenders of the trenches could have been enfiladed off into eternity. "Exactly so," went on the chief, "I foresaw that, and as I was'nt going to be blown into pieces because Hakaraia was a fool, I left him." Friend Penetaka is once more on good terms with his white neighbours, and is a very good fellow, though he did fight stubbornly against us.

From Tauranga southward we had of course to take to the saddle, and here let me give a hint or two to any tourist desirous of seeing the out-districts. Of all the mistakes which can be made for this kind of travelling none can be worse than to hire horses and wear breeches and boots. The screws one gets are not up to any weight; their paces are brutal, they mostly have sore backs, and they are bound to break down before half the journey is accomplished. A far cheaper and better plan is to buy at the outset and sell at

the end of the journey. Again, with regard to clothing:
breeches are an abomination: for there is always a good
deal of walking up and down hill to be done, and any tight-
ness about the nether integuments is exceedingly tiring.
Rivers, creeks, and small swamps abound; it is thus nearly
impossible to get through a day's work without wet feet, and
any one who has experienced it will know what a trial to
temper it is to have to pull off and on, day after day, long
boots which have once become well soaked. Pantaloons, as
loose at the knee as is compatible with comfort in the
saddle, good shooting boots, and leggings, form the very best
attire for travelling on horseback in New Zealand. Of
course the saddle will be a roomy one, with plenty of well
fastened D's; and then, with a blanket, or better still, a
'possum rug, in which are rolled up a spare flannel shirt, socks,
sponge, and toothbrush, strapped on in front, a waterproof
(long) just under the straps, a good supply of tobacco (for
that in the coast stores is vile stuff), and a small flask, the
traveller may jog along very comfortably.

It was about a four hours' ride to Maketu along a dreary
expanse of sand, though at low water the beach is hard and
fit for a canter; and, the Kaituna (eel eating) river ferried, we
were at the Arawa settlement of Maketu. It is strange how
nature has repeated herself about this part of the Bay
of Plenty; from the highlands of the interior, ridges
run to the coast, converging in their general direction, like
the spokes of a wheel, on the peak of Whale Island 12 miles
out at sea opposite Whakatane: between them flow rivers
which have gradually worn down the flanks of the mountains, have carried with their current and deposited the
detritus held suspended in their stream, and have thus
gradually reclaimed land from the sea, and formed, first
swamps, and then valleys which now boast of great fertility.
As a rule, the country over which the traveller is going to

pass may be easily anticipated: a river is crossed; then comes a hill, on the other side of which is a sandy beach with the ocean on one hand, and a shallow lagoon, or perhaps swamp, on the other; and so on. Again, Maketu, like Maungonui and many other hills on the East Coast, is a detached, elevated block of land surrounded by sea, swamp, and river. On its sea and river face the rock rises sheer from the water; and, about a quarter of a mile from the mouth of the Kaituna, the cliffs, lower here, are the site of a strong pa; near the centre of the block, a peak with its sides scarped away shews where stood formerly a redoubt, Fort Colville, inaccessible to an attacking party devoid of artillery. Close by the spot where the river falls into the sea a small grove of Karaka trees is shewn by the natives as a relic of their ancestors. It is well known that Maori tradition points to some island in the South Seas, called by them "Hawaiiki," as the spot from which the original migration to New Zealand took place in several canoes, each of which had a distinct name. That which touched at Maketu was called the "Arawa," and hence this generic appellation has been applied to the tribe inhabiting this district as far as Lake Taupo. The story goes that the chief of the immigrants, on landing, thrust the pole of the canoe into the ground, that it sprouted, and thus became the progenitor of the group of trees now in existence. Numerous other legends of the kind exist. For instance, at Kawhia, a harbour on the West Coast, an up-standing solitary limestone rock is firmly believed to be the original stem of the canoe "Taenui." As for Hawaiiki, its real position, and the truth of the immigration tradition, I believe there have been as many arguments and pamphlets on those subjects as originated from the antiquarian discovery made by dear old Pickwick at Cobham.

Some time ago the only hotel at Maketu was kept by a European whose wife, a half caste, had borne a rather conspicuous part in the war of 1863. Her first husband was a native, in arms against us, and she was in the Gate Pa on the repulse of the English, when she humanely administered water to the wounded who had been left there on the retreat. I cite this as an example that the natives are not always the ferocious savages they have been represented; in this case the warriors almost all belonged to the Ngaiterangi, whose boast it was that no white man had been murdered by them; and on this occasion they kept up their reputation. While on this subject I may mention that I was rather surprised at hearing one day a new comer gravely relate that the regiments repulsed at the Gate Pa could all night long hear the cries of their wounded comrades undergoing torture: and this was said in perfect good faith, and, but for my presence, might have been credited; the real truth being that Colonel Booth himself was the morning after the defeat found alive in the pa, and that the wounded officers and men had been placed by their foes in as comfortable positions as possible and supplied with water. I know that a personal friend of mine, mortally hit, was thus treated.

From Fort Colville there is a fine view extending over the horseshoe formed by the Bay of Plenty, the high mountains towards the East Cape, topped by Hikurangi, closing the view to the eastward; about the centre of the Bay, some thirty miles out at sea, a small cloud lying low announces that the volcano of White Island is in full operation; twenty miles to the S.E., Putauaki, or Mount Edgecumbe, backed up by the Uriwera highlands, shews its crater-formed head, in the hollow of which lies a dark, gloomy lake; to the southward extends a large plain, separated from us by a swamp traversed by a causeway, and growing nothing but fern; beyond the plain rises a low range of hills, a dip in which indicates our road to the Hot Lakes:

and to the westward stretches another chain, on the further side of which lies Orope, where we were watching the fantails a few days ago.

The Maketu Pa used to be a formidable affair. Built on a rising ground close to the river, it possesses on its landward face a natural steep glacis which has ere now been strewn by the bodies of fallen assailants; but even this and its fortifications have not always saved it. Mr Wilson's "Story of Te Waharoa" relates vividly some of the horrible incidents of savage warfare which took place at its capture in early days, even under **the eyes of** missionaries, helpless to avert the slaughter.

The pa is* entered at "Te Waharoa" (the principal gate), a rude pointed wooden arch, painted red, and adorned with fantastic and grotesque carvings supposed to represent the human face divine; the eyes are formed of the inner coating of the "pawa" **shell**, a kind of blueish mother of pearl; tongues loll out of wooden mouths; arms and legs are distorted and misshapen; the tattoo is imitated to the life; each spot on the posts **not** occupied by the figure of some ancestor is filled up with curiously carved scroll-work, and **over** the whole waves a fringe of pigeon and "kaka" (brown parrot) feathers. Once inside, we find the defence is twofold: along the crest of the glacis, with flanking angles distributed along the face and at the corners, runs a row of "manuka" **poles**, with thick posts at intervals of ten or **twelve feet. These** are all firmly imbedded in the ground, and lashed to **cross** pieces, the smaller stakes close enough together to prevent any object inside being aimed at by the assailants, but far enough apart, especially at the bottom, to allow the defenders to use their guns. About a foot and a half in rear of this fence comes a second, similar in all

* Or rather "was." At my last visit I found this gate had disappeared.

respects ; and behind that are rifle pits dug with a due regard to shelter from any cross-fire. These palisades are no
joke ; round shot and shell go through them like a bullet
through a pane of glass, leaving merely a small hole ; the
withes, made of split supplejack, are horribly tough, and a
party engaged in cutting down such a stockade while the
interior was held by a staunch hearted foe would be bound
to suffer heavy loss, and most likely meet with a reverse,
as we found to our cost in the old war in the North. Of
course there are innumerable legends of battles and slaughter
belonging to the place. One, which if I am not mistaken,
is mentioned in " The Story of Te Waharoa,"* is too characteristic to be passed over.

Some thirty or forty years ago Ngaiterangi and the
Arawa were at war, and the former occupied a pa called
" Te Tumu," situated on the sand hills on the way to Tauranga. This was surprised at dawn by the Arawa, and the
usual massacre took place. There were however some
fugitives, and a hot pursuit took place, during which a young
Arawa chief, who was foremost, perceived an enemy struggling to get through a swamp ; on rushing up to him he discovered that it was his own uncle : in this case, blood was
not thicker than water, and a blow with a tomahawk soon
dissolved the relationship. Now, the uncle was a well
tattooed man, even all down his back : so by way of a me-
mento, the graceless nephew skinned his victim, and with
the " rapé"† adorned his cartouch-box.

From such stories of violence and from their scene it was
a treat to turn away and follow a sheltered path leading to a
school-house occupied almost entirely by Maori children of
all ages, from sixteen to six. Just as we were going in, one
little brown imp came doubling out. " Hillo, my little

---

* Te Waharoa was a noted fighting chief of the Ngatihaua, and the
father of William Thompson.

† The tattoo on the lumbar regions is so called.

man, where are you off to?" asked one of the party.
"Fetch my book, me forgot!" answered the urchin in
English, to my surprise. I had however to go through
some more astonishment. The pupils were all clean, tidy,
and respectful to the master and mistress. Not a word of
Maori was allowed, except so far as to elucidate the meaning
of some puzzling English sentence. The reading was very
fair; the lessons in spelling, geography, and tables, well
done, one girl especially distinguishing herself; and the
writing was capital. **One task set** while we were there was
for each pupil to write out a piece of English poetry from
memory, and I am perfectly certain that the Upper Shell
at Harrow, when I was there, would never have turned out
such good hand-writing or so much poetry. The lines
selected were chiefly from hymns, but "God Save The
Queen" was also a favourite. The children are provided by
Government with bats, balls, &c., and some of the boys were
shaping very fairly in front of the wickets. I need not say
that we left highly delighted with what we had seen, and
ready to accord the greatest praise to the teacher, who, by
the way, informed us he did not know a word of Maori.

This was a good example of the new scheme of education
adopted by the Government in opposition to the boarding
system introduced by the missionaries. Even the stanchest
advocates of the latter can hardly deny that it has turned
out a failure; the theory was perfect, but in practice the
results did not justify the anticipations. It was supposed
that educating highly a few youths of both sexes, and then
launching the boys into the Maori world as native clergymen, &c., or putting the girls out to service, would be the
means of leavening the whole Maori lump; pity that such
an infinity of trouble should have been wasted : the expense
has been very heavy, and the consequences far from com-
mensurate. It is a well known fact that **many of the**

scholars who had distinguished themselves in these schools used their knowledge against their teachers, and that several have attained an unenviable notoriety in the records of Hau-Hau fanaticism.   The idea now is to try and impart to as many as possible of the present rising generation *some* education; reading, writing, the English language, and simple rules of arithmetic; some scholars will of course go further than others; but it is assumed, and very properly too, that the children who now learn a little, will, when they become fathers, be eager for the better instruction of their little ones.   Numerous day schools have been set on foot, and all over the North Island the natives are evincing an anxiety for the education of their children, and proving the reality of the desire by granting lands as endowments, and by subscribing for the erection of buildings.

CHAPTER VIII.

The Hot Lakes.

Mr. Trollope mentions the fact that before him two hundred writers have had their say about New Zealand; and as it is presumable that more than nine-tenths of them would not lose the opportunity of bringing in such natural curiosities as the Hot Lakes, and as he has followed suit, there has already been a fair amount of expatiation about these wonders of nature, so much indeed, as to leave little or nothing fresh to say about them. But any rambles in the colony are incomplete without a due process of parboiling at Rotomahana, and moreover my first visit to the Lakes was made under circumstances a little more exciting than those under which tourists generally see them, for on the shores of Rotorua actual fighting was going on between the friendly Arawa and the Hau-Haus.

In the summer of 1867 the latter had taken it into their heads to break out about Tauranga; my Orope friends and the Pirirakau led by chief engineer Penetaka were up in arms, assisted by a mob of fast young men from other parts of the country who wanted a bit of diversion, and who took to the amusement of fighting instead of wrenching off knockers and having rows with policemen as customary among their more civilised prototypes. The troubles commenced by a small party shooting an unfortunate settler who was going to set to work on his land; the rest con-

sidered themselves in honour bound to support their friends,
and a detachment of ours marching up a hill was fired upon,
the Sergeant-Major of the Regiment being killed; and so
presently we were all at it hammer and tongs. If my
description of Tauranga has not been of the vaguest, the
reader will remember that a belt of thick bush exists en-
compassing the open land ; and in this the Hau-Haus kept,
pouncing out whenever they saw a chance, and giving us an
infinity of trouble in marching and counter-marching after
them. We got up a contingent of friendly Arawa, and they
took well to the work. I saw them on one occasion clear a
bit of bush beautifully; without minding the fire we received on rising a bare hill leading up to it, they went in
just like a pack of fox hounds dashing through a small
gorse cover with the scent breast-high, and they did that
little piece of work very neatly, closely chasing the enemy
for about a couple of miles. But presently the Hau-Haus
found they were not doing much good about Tauranga, so
they bethought themselves that now was their chance for an
attack on the Arawa settlements on Lake Rotorua while the
men were away ; they occupied the forest which separated
us from these villages ; in fact they had interior lines, and
of these they availed themselves by quietly leaving our
vicinity and making their way to Rotorua by tracks which
have now given way to the main road from Tauranga by
Orope. So, while we were wondering what on earth had become of our sable foes, a cry for help arrived from Ohinemutu. In this case the longest way round was the shortest
way there ; we embarked at Tauranga, steamed to Maketu,
and set off to tramp up country on as hot a March day as I
ever remember. There was a great scarcity of water on the
road, and the first pool reached, some ten or twelve miles
from the kainga, was nothing but a nasty puddle of swamp
filth : so every one was pretty well done by the time we

reached the camping ground at Te Taheke, the ferry over the Kaituna river at the spot where it issues out of Lake Rotoiti.

Long before reaching this a peculiar fragrance manifesting itself every now and then as we topped a rise over which the breeze blew unimpeded warned us of our approach to sulphurous regions; and, on emerging out of the bush on to the shore of the Lake, we got our first introduction to volcanic agency in the shape of numerous thin columns of white smoke rolling upwards quietly and noiselessly out of the ferny slopes of the surrounding hills.

The next morning a short ride took us along the banks of Rotoiti, past the native kainga of Mouria, where we crossed a small stream connecting the two lakes, and brought us through a break in some low pumice cliffs on to the brink of the beautiful circular sheet of water known as Rotorua.

Opposite us on the further side, and at the foot of a lofty range of hills, there hung over the shore a misty vapour which, driven every now and then to one side or the other by an eddy descending from the gullies at the back, revealed the *whares* constituting the village of Ohinemutu.

Away to our right of this the hills sank down, till they ended in a low wooded range fringing the margin of the lake; to the left the country was open for a short distance, but a bare flat-topped eminence rising over bushy heights at a distance was pointed out as the trachytic mountain of Tarawera. From the centre of the lake sprung the gracefully shaped island of Mokoia, the scene of the oft-repeated legend of the Maori Hero and Leander; and from numerous points in the semi-circle formed by the shores to our left as far as Ohinemutu, jets of steam and volumes of white smoke curled up out of the ground. The great geyser, Wai Whakarewarewa, showed its presence afar off by a thicker and denser eruption of steam, but evinced, as far as we could see, no very peculiar signs of activity. Indeed it did not behave at all well during this visit, resolutely refusing to gratify our curiosity when we took a hasty look at it; once I saw it spout up; but as we were in full march back from a bloodless victory, and as it was some distance off, it could not be inspected so as to be appreciated. It was however well worth the ride to Rotorua to watch, as I did subsequently, the proceedings of the geyser as it took leap after leap in its periodical outbursts, each time attaining a greater height, as if it were testing its powers and gathering impetus for the final effort in which it shot heavenward a column of boiling water to an altitude of thirty or forty feet, again subsiding and leaving exposed to view the funnel from which it spouted, pierced down through a high cone formed by successive layers of matter deposited by the falling waters. There were plenty of other curious places around the geyser; clear pools, mud pools, &c., but my only chance of seeing them was during a flying visit when I had but little time to look around.

Shortly after striking the lake we reached the Ngae,* where of old the missionaries had planted an orchard the fruit of which was most acceptable on so hot a day. " Blessings on their souls;" for, if they did not, like the monks of yore, " brew good ale," yet wherever they set up their homes, their first care was to introduce English fruit trees.

From that we rode on ahead, now along the shores of the lake, and now on a pumicey track inland, till, near the village, green slimy puddles, with a thin film of vapour dancing over them, and each emitting odours far from similar to those in Atkinson's shop, began to grow more and more frequent. Pulling up in a bit of a square opposite the big *whare* appropriated as a Resident Magistrate's Court House, I found myself face to face with some four hundred Arawa

---

(reinforcements had come in from distant kaingas) who
started to their feet, gave three cheers *à l'Anglaise*, and then,
à la Maori, started off on the war-dance. It was a cordial
welcome, and thoroughly well meant; but I could not help
remembering that the crust of the earth about here was very
thin, and really the force with which the eight hundred or
so feet came thumping down together upon it seemed quite
sufficient to drive a hole through and create an unpleasant
cavity quite worthy of an earthquake. We were too late,
after all, for any real work; the Hau-Haus had made their
attack before any number of Arawa had mustered up; and,
cheered and excited by a female general, had established
themselves on a knoll close to the palisading of the pa.
This would never do; so a combined sortie of young and old
was made with much discharge of powder and many shouts,
and the enemy were driven off leaving their slain behind.
Discouraged by this unexpected repulse the Hau-Haus retired a few miles and employed their leisure in building a pa
which acted upon our friends just as a red rag does on a mad
bull, only they did not care about facing it by themselves.

After a few days all of us went at it, displaying such a
force of natives that the inmates of the pa very wisely did
not wait for our actual arrival, but retired taking all their
goods with them. Subsequently to our departure they returned, and, at the very spot where we had burned their pa,
a small fight occurred in which they were well thrashed.
Since then, with the exception of a skirmish which took
place when Te Kooti was being hunted by flying columns
in 1870, not one shot fired in anger has resounded along the
shores of Rotorua.

Of all the queer places I ever saw in my life, Ohinemutu
is certainly the queerest; it is a good sized Maori village,
the *whares*, among which are some tolerably large, following
each other in a sort of street along the little bays and in-

dentations of the lake, and comprising, at the time I speak of, one rather more elaborate than the rest, intended for the reception of visitors ; now, regular accommodation exists. Everything is of course pervaded by a brimstony flavour which soon however ceases to be noticed ; and the effects of the atmosphere and of the baths are visible in the shiny skins and bad teeth of the inhabitants.

Starting from the *whare-runanga* where we had been met by the population, we were introduced *seriatim* to some of the peculiarities of the place : turning round corner number one, there was a small open space, the "square" of the kainga, from a slabbed hole in the centre of which rolled up a quantity of steam curling round and almost hiding from view two old gentlemen who were squatting down contentedly and peacefully in this natural vapour bath.   A little further on, a brook, brawling down a slight incline, and partly concealing itself under the misty steam always hanging over it, was bridged by some rough flag-stones ; a few steps beyond this on each side yawned a deep black hole emitting a concentration of stinks, and disclosing a central mass of fetid boiling mud in a state of constant agitation, the orifice in the middle being every now and then closed and covered by a huge bubble which, bursting with a "B—b—b— lobb" let out a fresh collection of stenches ; it was just as if all the rotten eggs in New Zealand were being cracked at one and the same moment.

To a lazy man, Ohinemutu must be a paradise ; talk of the indolence of the Neapolitan Lazzaroni : pooh, they have to light a fire wherewith to boil their macaroni if the bajocchi are too scarce to allow them to buy their favourite food ready done. But here, the boiler is one of nature's providing : you put your kumeras, potatoes, what not, in a kit, tie a string to this, chuck the whole into a pool of water, and lie down by the side of your cauldron till the

viands are done. It is only the epicure in search of roast
meat who has to trouble himself about firewood; and, even
then, should his soul desire pork, he finds the animal ready
scalded and has only to slay and cook. It was really
amusing to watch the pigs luxuriating in the comfortable
warm mud at the edge of the black pools; there they were,
wallowing about in the height of porcine enjoyment, and, as
the first feeling of heat disappeared, giving first one roll and
then another, to keep up the temperature: by-and-bye however, there would be one turn over too many, piggy would
find himself in rather hotter quarters than he liked, and then
there was no end to the squeaking and grunting and
floundering about and general scramblification which would
follow; but master poaka in each case came out minus a
good many of his bristles; so after seeing a pretty constant
repetition of this little game, I came to understand how it
was that most of the Ohinemutu pigs walked about in a
hairless condition. All about the village these sights were
constantly repeated, and one small bay was literally a gigantic warm bath. The whole time we were there this presented a lively scene; it was always full of Europeans and
natives swimming about, racing, diving, ducking each other,
and disporting themselves like so many mermen, and mer-
maidens too; for, clad somewhat after the fashion of Biarritz
or Leuk, the dusky beauties of the pa frolicked in the water
as gaily as on shore.

About ten p.m., or half-past was our favourite bathing time;
the pool was then tolerably quiet and better suited to the
dignity of the "Rangatiras": we used to undress inside our
whare, stalk down with only a blanket wrapped round *à la
toga*, and rush in for a swim: the constant change of temperature was curious as one approached or receded from the
supplying fountains bubbling up below, some of them apparently more powerful than others, for there were spots

T

where a stroke brought one into water quite hot enough to
warn against a continuance in the same direction. Tired of
swimming, we would come on shore, light a pipe, and wade
out just far enough to allow us to sit or lie down on the soft
mud at the bottom.   But here there was occasionally a little
source of discomfort ; for every now and then a small jet of
steam would issue just underneath the bather's body and induce a rapid shift in his position.

The vapour arising from this huge warm bath, visible at
a long distance in the day time, settled down at night in a
thick mist obscuring all surrounding objects, and rendering
the shores of the little bay invisible even a few yards off, as
our Doctor found out one night to his cost.   He would stay
in after we had left, it was so jolly, and after paddling about,
when he struck out for home, there was no home to be seen.
His only guide was the temperature, as the cold water
meant the open lake ; but he had to be careful in avoiding
the other extreme.   At last he hit the bank, but at some
distance from the whare, and he had to tramp through a good
bit of the village in buff, arousing the wrath and dread of
several thousand curs, more or less, not then well accustomed to the sight of a man white all over.

We never found any need of towels ; the few yards walk
back to the whare were quite enough to dry us ; and, ye
Gods, how we slept after the bath !

The Ohinemutu natives are the proud possessors of a
magnificent war-canoe, " The Arawa," named after that
which brought their ancestors to the island ; and this was
made use of one day for the reconnoissance of a supposed
position of the Hau-Haus on the shores of the Lake.   It
was a huge thing, capable of holding about a hundred and
fifty men, and carved to a marvellous extent ; the very seats
were all adorned with scroll-work, and the stern and bow-
posts were composed of elaborately worked pieces of wood

symmetrically carved in a graceful open pattern and fringed
with feathers of pigeon and parrot. There were forty paddles on each side; three chiefs stood up on the seats; two,
sword in hand, the centre one wielding a taiaha; and off
we started, at first with a slow and steady stroke to the tune
chanted by these fuglemen: presently the measure changed
and the dips of the paddles into the water augmented in
rapidity, still keeping in perfect accord: at last the excitement of the chiefs attained its height; they waved their
weapons energetically with frantic gestures; they shrieked
out rapidly uttered guttural exclamations inciting to speed;
the paddlers responded, putting their backs into it at the rate
of ever so many strokes a minute, and the canoe hissed
through the water, a regular wave forming on each side of
her bows. All of a sudden, after a few minutes of such a
"spirt," the fuglemen would utter a shout, every paddle
was peaked simultaneously and struck by the oarsman with
the palm of one hand in such perfect unison as to produce
but one clap, and then down again each was dropped to re-
sume the original steady pace to the sing-song chant of " he
pu! he pu!" It was a curious proceeding, looking at it as
a passenger: from the shore it must have been a pretty sight.
The only approach to it I ever saw was the arrival of the Te ao
o te Rangi* canoe at Ngaruawahia on the occasion of Governor
Bowen's farewell visit in 1873. Standing on the point at
the confluence of the two rivers, and looking at the waka
racing up, it looked for all the world like a gigantic milli-
pede; the lofty stem-post adorned with long feathers waving
about like antennæ, and the height of the gunwale concealed
the rowers; so the paddles flashing in and out of the water
all together at a furious rate resembled exactly a lot of little
legs doing their utmost to bear along the huge body out of
whose sides they seemed to sprout.

---

* The light of the sky.

Not seeing anything from the canoe, we landed and climbed up a big hill, from the top of which the Hau-Hau position could be well looked into, without any exposure on our part, and we saw our friends going on quietly about their daily avocations and skurrying about the valley as if there was not a hostile pakeha for miles. I have a distinct recollection of arriving suddenly at the conclusion, while going down hill, that the way the chief in front of me, Pokeha, was carrying his double-barrelled gun was not quite safe; the descent was steep, he had the piece on his shoulder so that I was almost looking down the barrels, and both hammers were at full cock. Not to interrupt the march I made a pretence of a boot-lace being untied, stepped to one side, and took good care to interpose some half-a-dozen of our allies between myself and the chance of an accident. As before mentioned the attack made on the pa was fruitless; so, the enemy having disappeared, we gave ourselves a spell, and some half-dozen of us took advantage of the lull to canter over to Tarawera en route for Rotomahana. The road was not made then; it was a mere bush track in which our ponies had often to leap over fallen trees, and there was a fair amount of scrambling work along the broken path cut into a steep slope overlooking that exquisite mountain tarn "Tiki Tapu." Embosomed in a deep hollow surrounded by lofty hills whose rocky bases it washes, with barely a trace of beach anywhere, and with no visible or known outlet, this lake is an almost inaccessible pool the beautiful dark blue colour of whose waters suggests the idea of fathomless depths. The natives assert the existence in it of a "taniwha," that undefined monstrous animal belonging to their traditions: there may be one there, but we did'nt see it.

Before reaching Tarawera we passed another small lake—Roto Kakahi—having its exit in the Wairoa, a river forming a cascade near the Rev. Mr. Spencer's house which commands a most lovely view of the Tarawera Lake itself, and of the lofty, bare table mountain of the same name overhanging the further shore : to the right was heard the subdued roar of the Wairoa fall, while all around, in contrast with the scenes of beauty displayed by nature, a homely, well stocked and neatly laid out garden contained a quantity of English flowers, the verandah posts being festooned by a luxuriantly growing honeysuckle, which brought to mind many a walk in deep rustic lanes in the old country. There was no one at home, and so we committed a felony and helped ourselves to bunches of the fragrant flowers.

A friend of mine told me once of a rather curious coincidence which happened while he was surveying in these regions :—He had to erect a trig. station on the top of the Tarawera mountain, about three thousand feet in height, and started for the purpose with his native workmen. About half way up he observed that they carefully hid in a crevice of the rock the biscuit and tobacco they carried ; and, before he had time to ask their reasons, they requested him to do the same, lest he should offend the *Atua* of the mountain ; in which case they predicted the said *Atua* would avenge himself by fogs and storms. Of course my friend ridiculed the idea, and went on with his pipe. The moment he got to the top, a dense mist settled down, and no observation was possible that day, while the natives were ready enough with their " Did'nt we tell you so ?" The next day, the very same thing occurred ; but, odd enough, on the third trial, when by way of humouring his people he put away his tobacco, &c., no fog appeared, and he got all the sights he wanted.

At Kariri (Galilee) we embarked in a canoe manned by four strapping girls under the charge of a steersman, the males being all at Rotorua, and crossed the lake ; but instead of paddling up a narrow stream overhung with bushes which forms a connection between Rotomahana and Tarawera, and which is without doubt the capital of the kingdom of mosquitoes (and a densely populated capital too), we walked over the divide, a bare and hideous range of low hills, and had our first look at Rotomahana from above it. I think this is an advantage; on my next visit I took the stream; but the suddenness with which the view bursts upon the eye as one just tops the arid slopes is far more striking than the gradual revealment of the beauties obtained by emerging into the lake at the low level.

As to describing Rotomahana in a few lines, or even imparting in any way a full idea of its wonders, the task is simply impossible. All is so new and strange, the accompaniments to the scene of wood and water which lies at one's feet are so utterly unlike anything one has seen before, that all attempts at comparison are signal failures; photographs even, and I have come across some most faithful representations of the scenery, are far from conveying any correct idea of what the place resembles; they lack the colour, and no true picture of the Hot Lakes will exist until a first-class artist makes New Zealand his field of operations. And such a painter will find ample opportunities for his brush.

From the ridge on which we stood we looked down on a small lake, shut in by low hills in parts covered with brushwood, in parts open, and presenting slopes and terraces of various hues, from delicate pink to purple. About the centre of the lake rose an island of no great size, and the waters were covered with numberless duck and teal, protected by the Maori local law which forbids shooting over this splendid preserve.

The lake however is not itself the great centre of attraction. A hasty glance at it suffices at first, and then the eye is at once turned on the terraces, that to the left, and the nearest, Te Tarata, being the chief object of admiration, as

Otu kapurangi, the pink terrace, is scarcely visible from this spot. Imagine a shelving slope descending gradually to the margin of the lake in an uneven series of steps for some hundred and fifty feet, bounded on each side by low scrub-bush, and culminating at the top in an open crater, whence rolls out cloud after cloud of white steam. The steps appear from the height to be now white, and now purple, contrasting strongly with the azure hues of the basins, and glistening under the hot sun whose rays dance on the thin film of water constantly trickling down. At irregular intervals on the grades are pools;—pools! the word is a profanation; they are alabaster basins filled with molten silver, blue as the vault of heaven, over whose gracefully-recurved lips pours down with a gentle murmur a never ceasing flow derived from the boiling contents of the crater above. The more we gazed upon the scene, the more difficult it was to realise it, till at length one bold attempt was made at comparison, and H————* exclaimed that this must be the abode of the Queen of Naiads as it would be depicted by Grieve and Telbin in a transformation scene. To reach the Tarata we had to wade across the stream and then we found ourselves on a ripple-marked surface which crunched under every footstep just as if we were walking on so much sugar, and which on the margin of the pools lost its roughness and became as smooth as marble. These reservoirs, situated for the most part at the edge of the steps of this gigantic staircase, and resembling in the recurved shape of their rims the basins of the flower-vases in the transept of the Crystal Palace, contained luke-warm water; but each successive upward step as the terraces rose tier above tier increased the temperature as the distance decreased from the parent fountain. About half way up we reached the

---

* Since then shot dead, while gallantly heading a charge at the disastrous affair of Ngutu-o-te-Manu.

first really comfortable bathing place, and after undressing,
we began to have a dim idea of the comforts of a pilgrimage
with peas—unboiled—in one's boots.   The spiculœ played
the very mischief with our feet as we gingerly took the few
paces intervening between our clothes and the bath, but
then came such a header !   **Down** we went into the liquid
blue mirror, piercing, as **it were, through different** strata of
warmth, the water getting cooler **and cooler the** nearer we
sank **to the bottom,** and then we rose and swam round and
round, each bather's limbs looking through the intervening
medium blue as Marryatt's chalcedony statues in the Pasha
of Many Tales ; then we sat in turns on a convenient ledge
sticking out some two feet under water and smoked ; but
the sitting down part of the business had to be done with
caution, for, if any hurry was displayed, the cuticle was
bound to suffer.   The pipe finished, came another header
and swim ; then the water was voted cold, and all very
gingerly and tiptoedly made their way to a higher terrace,
and yet to a higher, till we ended by standing in a row
beneath the projecting lip of a basin, and receiving a shower
bath at a temperature which, if indulged in at first, would
have been simply scalding.   It was glorious, but slightly
enervating ; so we dressed and went on to the crater itself.
All this time we had of course been walking in water, and
this now was becoming so hot that we had to be careful so
as not to **let it over** our ankles ; we climbed through the
lowest lip of the crater, thereby getting into our boots a lot
of hot earth which was not pleasant, and we had a good look
down.   At first there was nothing but steam ; then came a
slight gust of wind which continued for a few minutes and
showed us a blue, still surface of water ; still for some
seconds ; then, bubbling and fizzing, the whole mass rose up,
and by a vent in the side discharged its over-plus to keep
full the basins below.   Sometimes, according to the natives,

this crater acts as a geyser, and sends up to a fair height a
column of water which must be of a huge size. Occasionally
it has been seen empty, and I have been informed that it is
possible at such times to descend into the hollow, and, looking down the funnel at the bottom, just catch sight of a
raging torrent of boiling water running along at a furious
rate.

It was on one of these rare instances, which detract entirely
from the beauty of the Tarata, that a hawk, now in the
Wellington Museum, was picked up in the crater, encrusted
with the sinterous deposit so completely that every feather
was preserved. Any object left to the action of these waters
speedily gets covered : I once saw a mouse literally cof-
fined in stone; and specimens of ti-tree branches and
berries, &c., thus acted upon are very common. At the
foot of the Tarata we entered a bit of ti-tree scrub where
Indian file was the order of the day ; to right and left were
sometimes mere hollows in the ground with thin wreaths of
steam floating out of them, sometimes villainous looking
little mud volcanoes, from one foot to three in height, each
furnished with a perfect crater and emitting a sulphuretted
hydrogen which would have delighted a lecturer on chemis-
try. Little upstarts that they were, they aped the customs
of their big brothers, and blobbed out their stenches with as
much self complacency as Tongariro could be expected to
possess when shooting out columns of steam with a roar
audible at a distance of a hundred miles.

It was getting dusk as we reached our camping ground, a
narrow ledge of seeming rock just on the brink of the lake,
with two or three *whares* situated near holes, nature's tea
kettles. Our meal was soon prepared : the potatoes were
tied up in a kit and dropped into the "Ngawa" (hot
spring); water out of this made our tea; we had brought
lots of cold meat, so we made ourselves comfortable. Pre-

sently the conclusion was universally arrived at that our resting place had not very deep foundations; the ground was very pleasantly warm, and, in sheer idleness, while listening to the "hakas" of our boat-women I whittled away at the rock with a bowie; of a sudden, in went the blade, and whizz! out came a jet of steam which made me jump up pretty sharp: there was just a rind about two inches thick between us and boiling water. It was some time before I could get to sleep: not for need of any blankets, but it did seem so peculiar to hear a confused noise of hissing and boiling just under head, and the thought would obtrude itself that possibly the weight might be too much for the thin shell on which we were reclining, and that we might find a way through a crack to regions below. However it did not do to express openly what each felt individually; and so, between fatigue and the somnolent effects of the numerous hot baths, we all were soon sleeping as comfortably as if there was not a drop of scalding water for miles. At daylight, every one was up, and a *kopapa* (a diminutive canoe) took us over to the island. Some people sleep on this during their visit; but, queer as we had felt our bed of sinter to be, yet there was in it some substance: on the island however, what with its general crumbliness and burnt out appearance, its tendency to let out suddenly jets of steam at unexpected places, and a sort of rumbling, choking and whizzing under foot suggestive of deranged internal machinery and of a possible sky-ward outburst, sleep would seem to be out of the question. The only "kainga moë"* comparable to it would be a piece of dough closing, in the absence of the legitimate lid, the mouth of a gigantic tea-kettle, well on the boil.

We had a look, and that was all, at the Pink Terrace; for stern duty called us away, and we were compelled to forego

* Sleeping place.

visiting the numerous nooks and corners around, all so worthy of thorough inspection. Of course we could not leave without another course of hot water at Tarata, and it was with a general regret at our inability to remain for a longer time that the nags' heads were turned campwards.

A few days later saw the little force marching back, the general feeling being, I have no doubt, fully expressed by a practical sub who openly avowed his regret at leaving a place where he got "half-a-crown a day field allowance for the pleasure of swimming in hot wather."

Before quitting Ohinemutu altogether let me not forget a duty hitherto shamefully neglected by tourists, and which I cannot pass over. Greenwich has its whitebait; so has Maketu; so in our favoured isle have also other places, where only the accompaniments of Mrs. Hart's cookery, brown bread, and iced cup are needed; but, Rotorua has its *kora*, a large prawn, or a diminutive fresh water lobster, whichever you prefer; he will taste as good however he be classed. My duty and pleasure consist in introducing my friend the *kora* in the fervent hope that some travelling Soyer may study him carefully and lovingly. Good, nay delicious, as the *kora* is when boiled, or steamed in a hangi au naturel, or even when knocked-up in a curry by the untutored paws of a bush cook, what will he not be when science has stepped in, when he has been made the subject of skilful gastronomic experiments, and when it has been decided in solemn conclave *à quelle sauce il se mangera.*

CHAPTER IX.

BAY OF PLENTY.

One of the discomforts of New Zealand travelling is that so much of the journey has, as a rule, to be performed along the coast line, and that such will continue to be the case until sufficient population has poured in to open up and occupy the interior. Such riding is pleasant enough when one gets on to a nice hard bit of beach for a canter of two or three miles, but a perpetual recurrence of tramps up and down over ridges, and of ploddings along a deep sandy shore, is exactly the reverse. The ride from Maketu to Matata— some twenty miles—was of the latter character. Soft sand, sometimes so soft as to be treacherous, through which the horses laboured heavily, put any pace but a walk out of the question; sand dunes to the right separated us from a dreary swamp; and to the left extended the vast expanse of the blue ocean, even on such a beautiful day as this swelling far out in huge rollers which advanced in a consecutive array of unbroken lines till the maximum height was reached, when the summits would curl over at one part, the curl extending rapidly to right and left and breaking into white foam as though old Neptune were firing a *feu de joie*, and then the whole would hurl itself with a deafening roar on to the steep shelving beach, and swish back again with a loud hissing noise. The sun was beating down on our necks, and the glare of the sand was painful to the eyes, increased as it was by the diamond-like scintillations sparkling up from the minute particles of iron which lie in black patches and form so large a component part of the beach. This is the Titaniferous Iron Sand of New Zealand which, found in millions of tons on the West Coast, is largely distributed over, or rather under, the whole North Island. In the days of bush fighting it used to be a common occurrence at the end of a day's march, when the maemae's* had been knocked up by the side of a stream, to see three or four of the men gravely set to **work** with pannikin, or the tin plate some carried in the haversack, and "wash" for a prospect; in the course of not a few marches I have seen many a bit of dirt panned out at what were supposed to be likely spots; and I never saw the black sand absent as a residuum, whatever was the soil thus dissolved in water.

About half-way to Matata the sandhills on the right cease, and give way to cliffs of indurated pumice sand on whose steep faces wind and water have combined to produce grotesque and quaint tracings, not very unlike the patterns adopted in the tattoo; at the back lies a goodly expanse of country, broken, but well adapted for sheep runs once grass has taken root in it and expelled the low fern now forming the sole vegetation.

Close to Matata we passed under the wide spreading branches of a magnificent old pohutukawha, whose flowers, now well out, made the whole tree a mass of crimson; and we presently got to the kainga itself, where dried eels, fried in shark oil, followed by a second course of rotted maize, seemed to be the delicacies of the season.

Of course there had been fighting about here in 1864 and 1865, during which the enemy had at first gained the advantage, penetrating as far as Maketu where the Hau-Haus very nearly got hold of the officer commanding while he was duck

---

* Maemae—A low hut worked up with sticks and interlaid raupo or fern, open in front, with roof reaching the ground on the windward side.

shooting. However, once opposite Fort Colville they learned that jumping about and singing out " Hau-!-Hau !" did not render them proof against pieces of 12lber segment shells; and they also had a fight with the Arawa in which they were well thrashed; so they bolted homewards lower down the coast. While the excitement was on, the Eclipse man-of-war threw sundry big shells at different pas, none however taking effect at the time. One 40lb. shell did not explode (a rather common occurrence with that calibre), and a native genius catching sight of the missile, and observing lead about it, made a prize of it at once. Here was a fine chance of getting material for bullets; so a big fire was made, the shell was popped into it, and a little group sat contentedly round smoking peacefully, and watching the melting of the lead. Shortly afterwards a " tangi"* was held over those of the party whose remains could be identified.

Some fifteen miles south of Matata, at the foot of a high spur of the Uriwera mountains which juts out here into the sea and forms Kohi Point, and spread along the banks of the Whakatane river, lies the settlement of that name. Formerly it was situated some four or five miles up the river, but the ubiquitous Te Kooti came down and laid siege to it. After a spirited resistance of two or three days, during which time the garrison was reduced to great straits for want of water, advantage was taken of an opportunity and the defenders made their escape.

Opposite the pa, on the other side of the river, dwelt an old Frenchman, Jean Guérin, married to a pretty half-caste woman, and father of a nice little girl, Mam'selle, as the men used to call her. Jean had a perfect armoury of weapons, but we rather gave him credit for bragging when he boasted of what he would do if attacked. He kept to his word

---

* Any one who has heard the "keen" in the south or west of Ireland can realise the "tangi."

though; with only two natives in the *whare* with him he managed to dispose of several of his assailants before a chance bullet killed him. The poor child was tomahawked, and the wife taken away.

The Kohi ridge is a pretty stiff climb, and on the other side of it exists a beautiful bay, just the spot for a quiet bathing-place, and celebrated throughout the neighbourhood for its pink water-melons. These are simply delicious: I know no greater treat, after a long and hot day's march under a burning sun, than to come across a patch of big oblong fellows which, when cut open, reveal a deep-hued pink mass ready to melt in the mouth, and then to set to work at the juiciest of the lot.

From the top of Kohi Point, where by the way native tradition relates that the Maori immigrants found on their arrival a pa occupied by aboriginals, is seen a fine piece of inland water, the Ohiwa, backed up by broken ranges in which have been discovered thick quartz reefs—whether auriferous or not is not yet known—and in whose centre rises an island on which the Hau-Haus more than once made their mark, the victim on one occasion being Mr. Pitcairn, a surveyor, who was most treacherously murdered. Keeping this to our right after descending the hill, another ten miles canter over a splendid hard beach brought us to the ferry over the stream by which it communicates with the sea. Thence for some miles we had to the right high cliffs covered with great Pohutukawha trees whose large crimson flowers spread a gorgeous carpet over the hill sides. Presently we forded the Waiotahi, not unmindful of the times when, if without an escort, we used to dash along here at full gallop, revolver in hand, in the fervent hope of getting safely past a spot where more than one ambuscade had been laid, and some with success. From this, a few miles ride brought us to the military settlement of Opotiki.

Opotiki is the spot where, in 1865, the Hau-Hau fanaticism got its first glut of missionary blood, and where its votaries inaugurated their conversion by hanging one of the very best friends of the Maori race, the Rev. Carl Sylvius Völckner, and outraging his senseless body in the most barbarous manner. The pulpit in the Opotiki Church, erected by his influence, still bears the stains of his blood left on it by Kereopa, the leading fiend in the whole matter, who has since met the fate to which he doomed his pious victim, and who preached from it a Hau-Hau sermon, with poor Völckner's head, flanked by those of two pigs, on the boards in front of him.

Vengeance was taken; an expedition of colonial forces was sent to attack the murdering tribe; and, after losing heavily in men, the Whakatoea were driven off their ancestral patrimony, which was given over to military colonists. This is one of the few places of the kind which have proved at all a success, though even here in only a small way. In riding over the flat lying between the two rivers which, issuing from the mountainous region at the back, enclose the plain, one does see pleasant looking houses, fenced fields, cultivations, and a goodly lot of stock, all belonging to original settlers: sights of prosperity, these, but too rare in military settlements in other parts of the country.

The whole of this district, from Whakatane southwards, was for a long time vexed and plagued with uncomfortable neighbours. The mountains of the interior were inhabited by the fierce Uriwera (a detachment of whom were the " Ake, Ake" people at Orakau), a tribe thoroughly hostile to Europeans, and whose boast it was that its fastnesses were a secure refuge against any foe; it was their common practice to descend to the coast down one of the gorges, shoot or burn, and then disappear as rapidly as they had come. In addition to the Uriwera, there also dwelt in the interior the

remnants of the Whakatoea, the tribe which had murdered
their missionary and had been driven off from their territories.
And so for a length of time the settlers had a good deal to
contend against, and had to be in constant preparation to
meet the foe. I cannot resist here giving one of many instances shewing the spirit which animated them. No need
exists to relate details; we were well in the glens of the
Uriwera, within five miles of a known strong line of rifle
pits which we had started to attack; the European part of the
force was but weak, and just at the last moment, after a
skirmish, my guide was induced to leave us. There was no
help for it, and I had to order a retreat. Directly the order
was promulgated, a private of the Volunteer Company with me
came up, and in the name of his comrades offered to raise a
subscription to persuade the guide to lead on again; and
this was in **a country where** it would be a mercy to a
wounded man to receive a bullet through his head, as it was
as much as twelve men in reliefs could do to carry one. Of
such a stamp were the men who formed the Opotiki settlement. It was in these deep gorges of the east country and
in the mountainous forests of the West Coast that the
colonial forces had their hardest work; for here they had
" Bush fighting" in reality. There were no roads, of course,
so there was no transport, and every one had to carry
his own provisions for four, five, or six days. No joke this,
in addition to blanket, rifle and ammunition, and in going
through country where the track lay up the bed of a torrent
which had to be crossed and re-crossed time after time, or up
steep forest-covered hills where projecting slippery roots and
a network of supplejack rendered any but the slowest progress impossible. Sometimes the way led over slopes clothed
with fern so high and so matted that the leading files had to
beat it down to make a track; and again, deep gullies barred
the way, spanned by a fallen tree forming the only bridge

across: and at every ford, at every bend of the streams, at every rise, at every difficult spot, there was the perpetual expectation of an ambuscade. An ambuscade in bush means this: a number of men are marching along in single file; leading them are a dozen picked scouts with senses of sight and hearing ever on the alert, who, with carbine ready in hand, minutely scrutinize each clump of bush, each fallen log, each boulder as they approach it. They turn a corner at a bend in the river; no sound betrays the presence of an enemy; but of a sudden, a cloud of smoke issues from the trees on the opposite bank, some twenty shots come hurtling through the head of the column, and, when all is over, it is found that one or two, or perhaps more, are past seeking shelter. And all this time not a glimpse can be caught of the nimble foe who has started off directly after delivering his fire; and who will be found a few miles further on awaiting at another favourable place the approach of the invading party.

Things are changed now at Opotiki. First of all, colonial forces penetrated the innermost recesses of the broken highlands; then the glens were swept clean by the friendly Ngatiporou under Major Ropata, and by Major Kepa's Whanganui natives. Most of the Uriweras have been brought down to the coast and are under surveillance of friendly chiefs; the remnant of the Whakatoea, the former owners of the country, have surrendered, are living close to Opotiki, and, by their extensive cultivations, attest their industry. Schools are also established, and I found the old feeling of hostility had quite disappeared, and that the men who, a few years ago, never met these natives but muzzle to muzzle, now fully appreciate their good behaviour, and are delighted to have them in the vicinity. Indeed, in the matter of road works, there is often a rivalry for contracts.

It was my fate to be concerned with Opotiki in its dark times, when the most violent sentiments in favour of a

" wiping-out policy" were naturally expressed by men who
saw that their lives and those of their families, and the
safety of their houses and crops, were daily in peril at the
hands of savages inhabiting the back ranges. In those days
the warning sound of the " Alarm" or " Assembly" was of
frequent occurrence; but now no ears were pricked up in
anxious expectation as to what the first note of the bugle
might portend, and the revulsion of feeling in the minds of
the settlers afforded a most pleasing contrast. Not the least
apprehension did I find among them of any outbreak ; they
were satisfied they could hang up their rifles except for
volunteer parades, and they were living on the best terms
with the natives, not only with the old friendlies, but
with those whom they designated as " the new lot :" i.e.,
the latest surrendered, who were the chief in rank and importance.

The wrecks of schooners still hampering the Opotiki river
testify to the former wealth of the natives who so stupidly
changed their faith for a whim ; but the memory of their
past comforts and the exhortations of Europeans are inducing them to pick up some of their old energy, and all along
the coast, south of Opotiki, and in the valleys inland, the
Maories are planting very extensively. The nature of the
country in this district is precisely similar to that described
in page 128 ; ridges running down to the sea and enclosing
valleys of more or less width. Some four or five of these,
separated from each other by steep ranges and leading down
from the interior, were apportioned out to military settlers,
but in the then disturbed state of the country, it was impossible for the allottees to actually settle upon any of the
lands thus set apart; the flat at Opotiki was the only one
really occupied, and there are consequently many thousand
acres of good land which some day will be turned to profit-
able account ; but, as in other cases, it will be necessary to

get them out of the hands of speculators who have picked them up at a cheap rate.

To any tourist who is fond of wild and rough scenery, and who does not mind really hard work, I would recommend a walk up any one of the gorges about here; the Whakatane for choice, which leads up to the Ruatahuna, the heart of the Uriwera country; thence the Waikarimoana lake can be reached without difficulty, and from that to Wairoa and Napier is easy travelling. The gorges are really fine; even when toiling up them with arms, swag, &c., it was impossible to help admiring the grand scenery which every now and then presented itself, and I doubt not that this latter must appear still grander to the eye of a tourist untroubled with the reflection that the next bend of the river, the next clump of bush, or the next ford may introduce him to a rattling volley.

It was at Opotiki that I had my second experience of the effects of superstitious fear on the natives. The first occasion was in the Ruatahuna valley, when, after a whole day's skirmishing and fighting our way up[*] we managed to get into the ancestral pa of the Uriwera, Te Tahora; just about dusk I heard a great hullabaloo, rushed out of the *whare*, thinking there might be some fresh Hau-Hau move, and found our native allies grovelling on the ground and singing out lustily. We were in a deep and narrow glen, and near the top of the wooded range on the right, a large ball of fire was slowly wending its way down the vale. It was quite round, seemed to be some six feet in diameter, emitted a dull light, and was unaccompanied by the slightest noise; presently it turned round a corner, and was lost to sight. The natives all would have it that this was the *Atua* of Te Kooti, and that it prophesied disaster to

---

[*] It was that morning that Lieut. White, in charge of the scouts, was shot dead in an ambuscade.

us ; however, except so far as some loss of life was concerned
in taking another pa the next day, it proved a false prophet.
Again, at Opotiki, at dawn one morning, my sentries saw a
precisely similar phenomenon, this time coming from seaward ; it sailed up the valley, and entered the Waioeka
gorge, when it was lost. There were a number of friendly
natives present on this occasion also, and I saw one of them,
a brave man, as I well knew, throw himself on the ground,
covering his head up in a blanket and groaning and moaning
in dread.

The inland track from Opotiki to Poverty Bay is now in
progress ; but when I knew the place well, taking that way
involved a very disagreable and rough journey ; so on this
occasion we decided to go by a schooner, pending the departure of which we rode a few miles to the southward and
paid a visit **to an old friend of** mine, **and a** staunch ally, Wiremu Kingi Te Tutahuarangi, chief of the Ngaitai, a small
tribe residing at a lovely little bay called Torere, where extensive cultivations attest the industry of his people. Wi,
(short for Wiremu) is rather a sharp fellow, and the way
he knocked up a bridge for me once showed considerable ingenuity. We were on the war-path after Te
Kooti, he with his people, I with some other natives
and a few Europeans. Taking different tracks we met at
the appointed spot, where, by-the-way, the enemy was not,
but between us rolled a foaming torrent, lately a fordable
river. The rain had come down, and we were jammed ;
the only possible way back was to get over to his side,
and cut a track through the bush along the cliffs. We
tried every scheme to cross ; I had a huge tree felled which
grew on the **edge of** the flat where we were camped ; no
sooner did it touch the water than it was carried away
like a straw. Then two or three of my natives very pluckily
swam over, one of them with a line between his teeth ; all to

no good. Meanwhile, I could perceive Wi was at work about something on his side, and presently we saw a lot of his men bring down a tripod formed of three poles lashed together near the top, and with the legs connected by flax leaves woven together so as to form a rough sacking. This tripod was planted in shallow water, secured by stones placed in the mat and round the feet, and connected by stout rails with the shore; another was deposited a little further on, and yet another; and it was perfectly marvellous to see the way the fellows did their work up to their chins, literally, in a rapid torrent. When it came to this, the deepest part, there was a mob of some thirty to each tripod; directly they had managed, with great difficulty, to carry it out and plant it in the right spot, a dozen of them would jump up and cling on to it, holding it down by their weight, while it was a race as to who should the fastest bring boulders to make it safe. Such a row as there was! Every one of the fellows was as naked as when born, and the way they leaped up and down in the water, and kept their footing, every now and then one of them being swept away and going down with the stream at express pace amidst the jeers of his friends, was something worth looking at; as fast as a tripod was down, rails were run out from that last secured and made fast to it; and all the time every man employed, and every one on the banks of the river not employed, was yelling and shouting out at the top of his voice; it would have made a capital subject for a painter, for the scenery around was very grand. In about two hours time communication was opened; we had to crawl sideways on a footrail, with another a little above it to hold on by; but every one got safely across.

During our Bay of Plenty trip we came across an old acquaintance who had started as a Maori trader at one of the villages; and I must beg the reader to fancy himself reclining on some bags of maize by way of a sofa, with the never-failing pipe in mouth, and a tumblerful of rum and water (the liquor drawn from the trader's private cask) close handy, and listening to our friend's **recital of his experiences.**   But, it is only fair he should have a fresh chapter in which to speak for himself.

CHAPTER X.

How we live in our Kainga.

To tell the truth we do not live very comfortably, but then, we have reasons which prevent our grumbling. Our dwelling house is composed of three adjoining raupo* *whares*, in one of which we sleep and eat, the centre one being the store, and the furthest the receptacle for unopened goods. We live chiefly on pork and salt meat and biscuit, and don't know what milk or fresh butter is. Our clothes are worth about twenty shillings the suit, and our beds consist of blankets laid on sticks stretched across a frame. So you have already some of the causes of our discomfort.

Jack and I (we are cousins) have been some time in the Maori trade, and a very fine business it is. We go on the principle of buying in the cheapest market, and selling in a very dear one. We dispose of our tobacco, prints, hair oil, blankets, &c., at a very fair profit; and when we buy corn, pigs, or potatoes for Auckland, we take care to beat the sellers down to the utmost; and then, pay them in "trade" which we have bought at auction for a mere song, and on which we naturally put our own price. Upon the whole I am sorry we are leaving off business; but people are so avaricious. Because *we* were doing well, others must needs come and set up an opposition—most demoralising this to the character of fair Maori traders—and as there is not room for two stores, as we are in honour bound not to reduce our

---

* Raupo—flax-rush; next to flax one of the most useful materials to the Maori which he possesses.

prices, and as besides we have already pretty well cleared out
all the cash of the place, and bought up everything the
natives have to sell, Jack and I have concluded to have a
shy at some other place.

Our kainga is situated in the centre of a half-moon forming a bay about five miles across from point to point of the
abrupt cliffs of the promontories. The pa is built upon a
slight rise, at the foot of which brawls a shallow stream
which, flowing from the interior, bends to the right, and
runs for about a mile parallel to the beach before meeting
a mass of rock which turns it sharply towards the sea.
Behind us, and on each side, rise high hills, clad with thick
bush, sheltering us from southerly and westerly gales.

Pleasant it is on a fine summer day to lie on the sward,
smoking the soothing pipe, gazing on the smooth bright face
of the unruffled bay, and listening to the ceaseless whish,
whish, and muttered thunder of the wavelets dashing
themselves to foam on the steep shingly beach. Just at
our back, and to either hand, on the flats at the foot of
the surrounding heights are the numerous clearings which
used to display plenteous crops of maize and potatoes, and
gladden our eyes by a prospect promising well for our pockets ;
a few fishing canoes lie motionless out at sea ; children
paddle about in the stream ; old women pass and repass,
laden with heavy bundles of firewood ; and mosquitoes and
sandflies bite freely, and eventually drive us to seek shelter
in the sea or in a shady pool of the stream. Now that is a
résumé of our daily life when not busy in the store.

Our pa is fortified in exact accordance with the most approved principles of Maori engineering, and although we were
really in a blue funk whenever Te Kooti's name was mentioned, we bluster much about what we have done for the
Government, and what we shall do again, when called upon
to draw half-a-crown a day and rations.

Y

We are rather a noisy and talkative population, and will sit and discuss every subject under its every possible or impossible aspect.

A stranger—a white man—passes through and stops to give his horse a feed ; at once some twenty or thirty people turn out, and squat down in all dignity, wrapping their blankets around them like so many Roman Consuls, smoke their vile burning torore (why they prefer that to our good strong black twist at 8s. the ℔, I can't understand), and take notes of every gesture. Then in the evening the whole thing is gone over again. What the pakeha said, what he did, how he looked, what he ate and drank, all is repeated for the benefit of the unlucky wights who were deprived of the pleasure of the sight. We are a cleanly race outwardly, for old Hakaraia, our head chief, is supreme, and has issued orders that the *kainga* shall be kept clean ; so, unlike most Maori villages, it would be difficult to find offal or refuse lying about in ours. Then constantly we go into the stream, and lather ourselves to a large extent ; but this, of course, cannot be expected except through the summer. On the other hand, there are one or two little things, connected with the person, which make me doubt the absolute cleanliness of our fellow villagers. We are not very particular about our clothing, though on certain occasions most of us can turn out in riding trousers at 35s., shoes and coats ; but our favourite costume by day or night is the blanket. When at work we use it as a kilt, and when walking, sitting, or lying down, we wrap ourselves up in it as if it were a virtue. We do a good deal of sleeping in the day time, consequently we talk constantly the whole night through, and are up betimes. When we go to bed we make up a big fire in the *whare*, roll ourselves up, close every possible aperture, and grunt or smoke ourselves to sleep in an atmosphere which, like the Strasbourg

ovens, would give a goose the liver complaint. We work
very hard—men, women, and children—in the sowing and
reaping seasons; but these once passed, we have a holy re-
pugnance to anything like labour. We like talking, we like
sleeping, we like sitting down gazing into vacancy; we are
fond of inane and indecent songs; we love gambling, and,
without the pipe, our lives would be a blank. There is
one other weakness I have not alluded to because it does
not come every day within our reach, but, when we see a
chance of getting at *waipiro*,* we don't stick at trifles. Our
favourite game at cards is *hipi*, a kind of brag, at which we
play for pins and matches; and, in the way of calculating amusements, we will beat at draughts the best player in
Europe. Our musical talent is not highly developed; but
we are great on that melodious instrument the Jew's harp,
and we grunt away at hakas: occasionally we get hold of
some English tune—say " Auld Lang Syne"—and distort it
to suit our voices and ideas of melody. Our food is not
very varied. Fish, potatoes, and kumeras constitute the
staple; while luxuries are occasionally indulged in in the
shape of rotten corn or eels stewed in shark oil. We have
heaps of pigs, but we sell them, and are too lazy to milk
our cows. We hoard up carefully any money we have, are
precious sharp at a bargain, and are very distrustful of every
one. Amongst us there exists an individual called Matiu,
whom Jack has christened " The inspector of Weights and
Measures." When we first came he was always pottering
about the store, and every day gaining information about
our scales. Now that he is perfect in them, not a pound of
sugar can be bought without his being brought up to ascertain that we weigh it out correctly, and he is particular to a
hair's breadth. Talk of doing a Maori indeed! It would
take three Armenians to swindle him; and an eastern pro-

---

* Lit. Stinking water; alias, spirits.

verb runs that it takes three Greeks to do an Armenian.
What I like about the people of our *kainga* is their utter
absence of shame in asking for things.   Among them are a
few "rangatiras," pretty well off; but even some of these
will beg for anything they see like the veriest "taureka-
reka."* Old Hakaraia attended the other day a *tangi* down the
coast over the remains of a cousin. . He was of course much
affected—snuffled and whined after the most approved
fashion, and shed several pints of tears.   The division of
the property took place, and to his share fell a very smart
sound whaleboat, complete; so up got the old man, and,
enumerating the different degrees of relationship he stood
in to the deceased, and his appreciation of his virtues,
" *tangiéd* " again to such an extent, that another relation,
affected at his extreme grief, presented him with a horse.
"Ah ! that's very well, " quoth Hakaraia, " but what's the
good of a horse without saddle and bridle ?"   These were
brought brand-new from a store; and then the old humbug
expatiated so largely on the hard-up state of his hapu that
he got, in addition, a present of a whole lot of clothing;
and didn't he grin with delight when he returned with his
gifts ?

Last Christmas he gave it out as his intention to abolish
drunkenness, and it was arranged that neither he, nor the
other rangatiras, nor the native policeman, were to enter
the store by day, but he tipped us the wink to keep some
decent liquor for the evening.   We sold that day over twenty
gallons of rum; and as fast as a fellow tumbled down he
was lugged out by the policeman and tied to a flax bush.
But didn't Hakaraia and the bobby make up in the evening
for their enforced sobriety by day !   Only the other day old
Hakaraia came to Jack with a very grave face.   It seems
the garrison near us were getting up games, including a

---

* Slave; common person,

canoe race, and had sent down for subscriptions: "I don't mind putting my canoe in" says Hakaraia, "and paying the entrance fee; but if I subscribe to the races, and my canoe does not win, will my subscription be returned?"

Among our chief nuisances are dogs,—curs rather. They abound in our kainga, are inveterate thieves (and if **we** kill one there is the deuce of a shine), and growl, snap, and bark at all hours; they have made us pass many a sleepless night. We have spent an exhilarating day in doing nothing. Times being slack, perhaps we have sold a few shillings' worth of flour and tobacco; we have nothing to read, and we have talked over every possible topic; so we have gradually smoked ourselves to sleep, thankful that there is at last some occupation. **All of** a sudden a yelp is raised by a dreamy cur; and from every corner, from under the eaves of our *whare*, and from every hole about, an answering chorus arises prolonged in a hundred distinct **howls**. Gradually this sinks, and just as we are thanking **our** stars it's all over, some morose and discontented cur gravely stalks into the open, and, jealous of the repose enjoyed by his friends, opens his jaws and gives vent to a melancholy yelp. Instantly again commences the universal charivari, which is only quelled by leaping out of *whare* doors, and with many an "Ah—ta" and "D—n" discharging sticks and stones at the brutes. Talking of *whare*-doors, I don't think, now that I have lived in a Maori *kainga*, that I shall ever wonder at the phenomenon of the reel in the bottle. I dislocated every joint in my back bone before I properly understood the method of getting into a Maori *whare*. You first of all stoop down and bend forward, loosening your **spinal** process; then you put your right hip out of joint, advancing it into the *whare*, at the same time giving your neck a crick; you then make a violent shoot forward, and, if the *whare's* high enough, spring up

and hear all your joints clicking back into their normal
position.   On one occasion Jack and I went a little way up
country to buy produce, and were given a shake-down in a
big *whare* where by chance I took up my berth underneath
the window (an opening with a sliding wooden shutter).
By and by men and women flocked in and a fire was lit :
this was bad, but as I resisted every attempt to close the
window it was endurable. I went to sleep, and had troubled
dreams ; I remember fancying I was in the black hole of
Calcutta ; then I imagined myself in a much hotter place ;
and lastly, I awoke with a choking sensation, perspiring at
every pore, and panting for breath. All was dark, and the
mephitic air was stifling ; as soon as I regained partial con-
sciousness, I felt for the shutter ; it had been closed during
my sleep ; hastily I slid it back and thrust my head out.
The best claret cup I ever drank after a long innings on a
hot day was nothing as compared with that delicious draught
of pure mountain air.

We have among us some half-castes, chiefly girls, who
speak English pretty well. A few of them were educated
in Auckland, but prove the old saw of " what's bred in the
bone." They are as much Maori as the oldest *waihine* in
the place, the only advantage they derive from their education being the doubtful one of being able to translate for
ignorant visitors the very questionable conversations and
songs going on. For we are by no manner of means a moral
people, though outwardly most religious. Every morning
at daybreak I am roused by the tinkle of the bell summoning
the pa to Protestant and Catholic worship, and every evening the ceremony is repeated ; while on Sunday the bell
rings so often that I am reminded of the saturnalia of clangs
at Oxford. But, these religious attendances notwithstanding,
our talk and morals are of the loosest, with the exception of
the married women who are rarely known to break their vows.

Not far from us exists a military post; but, notwithstanding that we have much traffic with it, we are far too lazy to do anything to the road, though it leads by staircases up and down two high ranges. If a tree falls across the track we go round it even though it entails a steep ascent; but we don't care; it's only our horses who suffer. Poor beasts! we saddle them at two years old, ride them at full split along the level, push them up the steepest hill, and never consider a sore back. **We** are good riders too. With a strip of flax for a bridle, without any girths, and with the stirrup iron grasped between the toes, we go at full gallop and turn corners which would, under the same circumstances, shoot **many a** fox-hunter out of his seat. On these rough ponies of ours we are pretty expert at galloping after young stock, catching their tails, and twisting them over. **On one oc-**casion while getting in some beasts for us, the Maories got a **heifer** thus and tied her feet up. There she died. So Jack Maori immediately **said** he would eat her, as meat would make him very "maroro" (strong). There was an old tin lining to a box at hand, and on pieces of this bits of flesh were singed in the flames, and hastily devoured. Two white men were passing through that day, and, on our return to the pa, they thanked us for the fresh beef we had sent them. **Jack** looked at me, and I at Jack. "But," said one of the fellows, "I don't think it was properly bled; it tasted queerish." We saw at once what it was, and **as** soon as we could for laughing, told them they had partaken of a dead heifer. They rushed off, and in a quarter of an hour came back with very pale faces begging for **a tot.**

It is a very curious sight to see us performing hakas.[*] We, the Ngatikoreros, consider ourselves the best hakaing tribe on the coast, and we are constantly practising. Two or three young men or girls cannot sit down without presently

---

[*] "Haka"—native choruses.

going through the pantomimic gestures. Sometimes a Government swell visits us, and we give him a treat. Of course we have the war dance first of all after the inspection of arms, and this is more easily imagined than described. In fact, a genuine war dance is enough to shock the feelings of any one, and I have seen more than one which would frighten the most enthusiastic praiser of the noble savage. The haka is of course in many cases as bad; but in many others it simply consists of songs relating the deeds of departed ancestors, chorussed with a series of guttural intonations and accompanied by contortions of the body, quiverings of the hand, and distortions of the features. Many a time have I smoked my pipe in a large *whare* full of young fellows squatted down, stripped to the waist, the perspiration pouring off them from their exertions ; every muscle quivering, and every motion of head, body, and arms carried to such precision that the whole seemed moved by one wire. In the claps of the hands, a frequent feature, the ear could distinguish but the one sound. One pretty haka they have, in which each performer holds a ball with a short piece of string attached, and the different motions given to it with great rapidity and in perfect time form a pleasing accompaniment to the monotonous dreary sing-song recital. At times the voice seems to proceed from the heels, it is so deep. As a rule, we are a graceful race in our gestures, and, as we have a language of signs, we hardly speak without an amount of gesticulation which would delight a Frenchman. Nothing can be more imposing than to see a tall, stout, elderly chief, robed in blankets and flowing shawls, which add so much to the human figure, impressing his ideas on his audience ; occasionally as he gets excited and wishes to collect his thoughts, he runs forward a few paces, gives a series of leaps, repeating his last words, and then stalks back to his starting point to go on again. The worst of it is that, once

speechifying begins, it goes on almost for ever, and the
dignity and grace of the speakers are forgotten in the excess
of loquacity. I have just been reminded of one period of
our existence when it rained for a fortnight. We had but
two books,—an old arithmetic and a Maori grammar; but
there were lots of eggs. So all we had to do was to beat up
an egg in rum, drink it, smoke and sleep for a few hours,
and then repeat the dose. After a week we could not stand
it and we tossed up for who should have a holiday; I won, and
when I came back I found my cousin looking like a ghost.
He swore he wouldn't pass such a time again for all the
profits to be made out of the whole Maori nation. On the
whole I must say that the days we spent in our kainga
passed away miserably slowly; the only sport was pigeon
or duck shooting, both tame work, as the ducks have to be
stalked, and twenty pigeons can be got without stirring from
under a tree; but in the season these are delicious eating,
especially when they are feeding on miro berries, when they
have a peculiar aromatic flavour. They are beautiful birds to
look at, with their green and gold plumage, and they are nearly
twice the size of the home pigeon. The red-billed pukeko
makes very good soup, as rich as hare soup; and curlews in
winter form a capital dish. We tried a shag once, bury-
ing the bird for three days, and it wasn't so bad. Our
best fish are the tarakihi, patiki or sole, and whitebait. In
June and July we devour the latter by the thousand,
although we lack the lemon, the brown bread and butter, and
the iced cup of the Trafalgar. I never could bring myself to
shoot the pretty tuis (parson birds), though Pakeha-Maories
aver them to be delicious, neither could I ever relish the
brown kaka, the New Zealand parrot. One thing we have
good, potatoes; and our method of cooking them in a *hangi*
is first-rate; this is the way. Dig a hole in the ground, fill
it up with dry sticks, set fire to them, and shovel on lots

z

of small stones : these of course will get well heated, and, when they are hot enough, cover them with large dock leaves.   On these you place your scraped potatoes, kumeras, pumpkins, or what not ; cover these also carefully with leaves, on the whole pour a couple of gourds of water, and then heap on earth till not a jet of the steam thus generated by the red hot stones can escape. In forty-five minutes, dish up, and you will say that not even in the most potatophagous parts of Ireland have you ever had more " maly spuds." Of course in former days these *langis* were occasionally made of a size sufficient to cook something more than potatoes, but that was on swell occasions only.   However, I have seen a small porker prepared for the table in this way, and it was uncommonly nice.

As a conclusion I may say that our existence since our start in the Maori trade has been like Cowper's traveller— " remote, melancholy, slow."

CHAPTER XI.

TE REINGA.

From the summit of Maketu Hill we just discerned a cloud-like appearance far out at sea, denoting the position of an active volcano, and in riding along the arc of the Bay of Plenty we have approached nearer and nearer to it, so as to be able to make out that the smoke issues from an isolated cone-shaped island rising in dreary solitude from the depths of the ocean; only twelve miles off Whakatane a somewhat similar peak exists, Whale Island, but no longer active, the only volcanic symptoms now about it being its shape and hot springs. But White Island is still a true volcano. I never landed on it, though many of my friends have done so; one of whom, by the way, discovered that slipping through a thin crust into boiling sulphurous mud was neither a pleasant nor yet an efficacious remedy for the gout. I once however steamed slowly close past, and was enabled to see that it was a burnt out, bare mountain, with hardly a trace of vegetation on its sloping sides; to the southward, the lip of the crater had given way, and the opening thus formed allowed us to judge easily of what the interior consisted. We could see a green, slimy-looking lake over whose surface curled the same kind of vapour that we had so often seen at the Hot Lakes; the interior slopes were steep, and apparently composed of rocks rotted down by the incessant heat; from numberless nooks and crannies spurted up jet after jet of steam; here and there yellow patches denoted the existence of masses of sulphur, sufficiently distinguishable indeed by the smell; and, over all, hung as it were a sense of utter desolation. It had a weird and grim aspect, this bare azoic rock, shooting up 850 feet above the calm blue sea which broke in ripplets on the small lava reef at the base, and sending its roots a hundred fathoms down to establish a volcanic communication with Tongariro by the chain of solfataras, &c., extending right up to Taupo. Had it been formed during some fierce submarine convulsion? Or was it rather the wreck of some mighty peak which had in past geologic ages towered over a range in a now submerged Austral Continent? Submarine or terrestrial by birth, it forms a most striking, but most sombre and dismal feature in the scenery of the Bay of Plenty.

By a piece of good fortune, after leaving Opotiki we kept fair weather on both sides of the East Cape, a rather unusual occurrence; and, after sailing along for a couple of days with a high broken coast on the right, we caught sight of the first land seen by Captain Cook in these parts, Young Nick's Head, a high white cliff which forms the southern promontory of Poverty Bay. If ever there was a misnomer given by discoverer to a spot, it was the above name; but in justice to Captain Cook it must be said that the first impressions of Turanganui, even now, are not favourable; for the township is built on a sandy soil, the road leading inland is ankle deep in sand, and every breeze carries with it clouds of blinding gritty dust. The town is however nothing; it is in the country at the back that all interest lies, and once the tourist gets three miles out, he soon sees the difference.

Poverty Bay, indeed! Not even when scathed by fire and sword, as I first saw it; its settlers slain; its houses burnt, blackened stacks of chimneys only remaining to indicate the sites of once happy homes; its orchards and gardens ravaged; its cattle slaughtered; and indices of murder and rapine meeting the eye to right and left; not even then did it deserve the name. I had never before seen such rye grass as that through which I rode, up to the horse's girth, over the Patutahi plain; in the ruined gardens huge vines still trailed over the few buildings which had escaped the general destruction, or lay thickly matted on the ground; fruit of every description was in abundance; in the Bishop's orchard, near the old Episcopal residence, school and industrial farm combined in one at Waerangahika, then all deserted and the shell of the house riddled with bullets poured into it during the old fight in 1865, the plums, (unripe!) were weighing down the branches; and as for apples, they were literally being carted away by loads.

That was in 1869, and we had not then much opportunity for sight-seeing; of the few families which remained in the district none resided beyond the township, for Te Kooti and his crew were still in the field; he proved it to us too, by issuing out of the gorges just in time to assure us he was still full of mischief, notwithstanding the mauling he had received at Makaretu from Major Ropata's Ngatiporou, and we had to follow him up to Ngatapa, and have it out with him there.

Since then it may be said that no place in the Northern Island has advanced at such a rate of progress as Poverty Bay. In 1869, its population was about a couple of hundred, and its run holders had not extended far beyond Waerangahika; now it numbers about thirteen hundred souls, and the back country is being taken up even along the line of road which is in course of formation between it and Opotiki. Even the mountain on which stood Ngatapa pa, taken by Colonel Whitmore's colonials after three days' siege in 1869, is now included in land which will shortly be occupied by sheep.

Before taking a ride round previously to continuing our

route, it was the proper thing to visit two natural curiosities which may be called the lions of Turanganui. A few hundred yards from the hotel a tidal creek falls into the river which forms the harbour, and at low water the bottom of the former is found to be a soft sandstone on which sundry queer markings had been for some time observed. I believe it however was the Ven. Archdeacon Williams who first paid attention to these and set to work to make them out. As a reward for his trouble he was enabled to obtain numerous perfectly preserved moa foot-prints, in some cases finding it necessary to shave off a superincumbent slab, while occasionally the marks lay quite distinct on the surface. Those which were discovered have been taken away, and no more are visible at present; but there is every probability that a search under the sandy banks of the stream would disclose more. At all events I found that a little rubbing with the finger on the friable sandstone produced a very fair imitation of the genuine article.

The other lion is a petrifying spring on the beach the further side of the main river. We crossed in the boat and landed on a reef composed of a peculiar and disagreeable kind of rock. Its Maori name is "Papa," its scientific appellation I know not; it is blueish in colour when dry; gets reddish under water; delights in running in ridges and furrows, the former inclined at an angle; and is, when wet, far more slippery than any well prepared ball-room floor. It was my luck once to ride northward from Poverty Bay to Waiapu, about a hundred miles, and back; and, when I was not leading my horse up or down steep, high, and almost trackless hills, or occasionally getting a canter on a bit of sand, I was going over acres of this horrible stuff. At every point, in every little bay, jutted out the uncompromising reef; occasionally it was just as much as we could do to get round a bluff between the waves, and that was about as nervous work as could be; for a fall on the jagged edges of the rock would have been no joke. Luckily, mine was a *hoio whenua* (country bred horse), and the manner in which he picked his way was beautiful. About a mile along the beach after crossing the river we came to a cliff, in which there was not apparently much to distinguish it from any other cliff—but, a couple of blows with an axe soon showed a difference. There had evidently been a groove here once filled with flax, and down which had run a stream rising from some spring in the limestone rock. How long the stream took about it, it is impossible to say; but the hollow is filled up, there is only a trickle of water; and, what was flax is now stone. We hacked away and got out specimens of every kind, from delicate leaves and shoots to coarse masses; lumps looking just like a breccia of bird-bones; pieces of stalk and roots; leaves curled up slightly, or else completely rolled round; and the greater portion of the whole was thoroughly turned into stone, the very leaves, when broken across, showing the petrifaction.

There are plenty of directions in which to ride from Turanganui. Eastward, along the beach and by the mouth of the "Big River," the Waipaoa, lies the coast way to Wairoa; a road formerly of climbs and slips, and productive of groans, weariness, and bad language: now however it is improved. In a more southerly direction lies the inland track to Wairoa, by Te Reinga, the route we are bound to take; and, beyond Waerangahika, to the westward runs a long valley, breaking up into others, and into which falls the road from Opotiki.

There can hardly be a pleasanter ride than to start early, as we did one fine morning, canter out to Patutahi and ascend Pukeameonga, a small conical hill in the plain, and have a look round. From this a view is obtained of the whole level of the Bay, from Nick's Head to Turanganui, the former being the prolongation of the low chain which sweeps round the southern edge of the basin, and through gaps and passes in which access is had to the interior. Turning our backs on Turanganui we had to our left the dark Pipiwaka Bush ; and beyond it the sea, the river, and a series of rolling hills ; to the right the view extended up the Waerangahika valley, and just in front gaped in the hills a well known opening, for the mouth of which we once had a tidy race with some of Te Kooti's people. From Pukeameonga we had caught sight of a party of Hau-Haus creeping along the foot of the hills after a plundering raid, and it fell to my lot to ride down and hasten up our men ; it was not pleasant galloping, as the thick rye grass concealed a quantity of holes in and out of which my horse kept blundering, but the falling was pretty soft. It was then a case of "swags off" and "doubling ;" but the Hau-Haus had the start, and by throwing away their *pikaus* (loads), managed to get first into the gorge, up which we eventually followed them on the march to Ngatapa. That day, whichever way one looked nothing but ruin and desolation met the eye, and the only people about were armed men. Now there was a difference. Roads crossed the plain ; houses were dotted all over the country, built, or in course of erection ; miles of fencing were visible ; cattle and sheep roamed about in numbers, and all looked prosperous. It speaks volumes for the district that it should have so well recovered from the crushing blow it got while in an infant stage ; and I doubt if any scene in New Zealand could give to one who had seen the place under both aspects a better realisation of a picture of Peace and War than the view from Pukeameonga. From the hill, we cantered across the flat, where clover is now assuming the place of the old luxuriant rye grass, and, after fording the river, rode on to

Wairangahika. Alterations here also are to be seen. Once more is there found a good substantial gentleman's residence, approached along an avenue of glorious willows, and surrounded by well fenced and well kept paddocks; and a couple of miles further we arrived at the station of the Armed Constabulary, the military township of Ormond. The military settlers here at all events have not got one of the grounds of complaint which are heard elsewhere; they cannot grumble at the quality of the land; and some of them, either in person or by substitutes, are working away effectually at it. Beyond this again stretches a long valley in which some miles up are found springs exuding petroleum for the exploitation of which a company has been formed; and the whole of this is being rapidly taken up by runs, the influx of genuine settlers into the district promising well for its future prosperity. Its last, but not least advantage, is the climate, without a doubt the pleasantest in the North Island.

There is yet another most interesting ride to take —to Whakato, where is to be seen a specimen of Maori carving, in which the Ngatikuhungunu (Poverty Bay natives) used to be very proficient. Formerly there was to be found in Poverty Bay a council chamber, the upright slabs of which inside the house were of a black, tough wood, and wonderfully carved with all the grotesque imagery of which the Maori sculptor was so fond. This house was taken possession of during the war, and now forms a portion of the Wellington Museum. There is however a specimen still to be seen at the abandoned mission station of Whakato, and we went to look at it; a few miles out of Turanganui we were ferried over the Waipaoa and found ourselves in a magnificent old orchard in the centre of which stood a high barn-like building, evidently a Maori church. Broken windows

2 A

a ripped-up floor, and holes in the roof shewed that
its glory as well as its parishioners had departed; but the
huge carved slabs still remained entire. I think they were
a dozen in number, about eighteen feet high, and carved to
represent each some departed *Taipuna* (ancestor). The
amount of work expended on them must have been wonderful, and it must also have been no slight task on the
ingenuity and nature of the workmen to refrain from insert-
ing any of the peculiar touches which usually characterize
Maori carvings; however, as the slabs were for a church, it
was necessary to keep them free from anything approaching to the general style.

I have briefly alluded above to the Poverty Bay massacre;
there is in connection with it an anecdote which is worth
relating as exemplifying a noble trait in the Maori character.
Awakened by the news of the ruthless work proceeding
around them when Te Kooti and his band fell upon the
settlement and destroyed it, and flying in haste to a place of
refuge, a small party of Europeans passed by a hut where
were sitting an old Maori and his wife, both well-known to
them. A short time afterwards a number of Te Kooti's
men arrived in hot pursuit and questioned the old man as
to the direction taken by the fugitives; he declined to
answer; threatened with death, he still refused to betray his
friends, and was at once tomahawked. The savages then
turned on the wife whom they had widowed, but she was as
faithful as her murdered husband, and sent the pursuers on
a wrong track. Acts of ferocity are loudly blazed abroad;
deeds like the above are but slightly noticed; yet such an
instance of self-devotion merits record as much as any act
of heroism mentioned in history.

There are two ways of getting from Poverty Bay to Te
Wairoa, the next settlement to the south; by the coast
line, or by the inland track. The latter was the one I

adopted, chiefly with the object of getting a view of "Te Reinga."

This name applies properly to the "Hades" of Maori mythology, supposed to be somewhere beyond the North Cape. The tradition ran that out of the cliffs of this promontory grew a huge tree, from the branches of which the souls of the departed took a final leap into the other world, there to lead a *dolce far niente* sort of existence, without cares or occupation. Curious, that the highest aspiration of a people should be a hankering after the life of a vegetable!

We started one summer afternoon and, after passing through the plain, got into a very good undulating sheep country which lasted for some miles; camped by a little stream, and the next morning entered upon rather more difficult regions. After riding for a little distance through an open valley, we found it of a sudden close in, and we descended a steep slide into the Huangaroa, a river with a bed of papa rock. It was absurd, whilst on the bank, to watch the floundering of the horses as they slid and stumbled about on the greasy ledges, their hind quarters one moment well out while they were up to the shoulders in a deep hole; then sometimes all four hoofs seemed to go away in different directions all at once, and the poor brutes looked like awkward skaters in trouble and aware of the imminence of a tumble; and then the riders' faces! It was a case of sticking on "all one knew," and every feature expressed uncertainty as to whether the next minute might not inflict the thorough ducking which two of our party got. To this moment I cannot recollect exactly how I scrambled across, as every instant I felt my horse going, but he managed to keep himself up somehow or another. Then came a climb, a descent, and another crossing of the same river over the same kind of stuff: then we were on the hills. Had it not been for the name of the thing, we might as well have had

no horses, for they were of no use here for riding purposes—
it was quite a case of "here we go up, up, up, and here we
go down, down, down." In one of the latter we came upon
a lovely little nook : the river had cut its way through high
cliffs of a white chalky looking stone, and at a sudden turn
had scooped out a hollow, now clothed with grass and
shaded by peach trees ; once down in this it was impossible
to tell how to get out again, or even to see which way the
river entered or left : altogether it was a charming spot for
a pic-nic, and here we lunched. While mooning about during
the post-luncheon pipe, I was astounded at the quantity of
fossils to be seen ; every boulder was a mass of shells, every
pebble bore on it the imprint of some former denizen of an
ancient sea ; for the specimens were all marine, and, as far
as I could judge, of forms identical with those now found on
our shores.

Topping the hill on the further side we got a grand view.
Close by to the left rose a magnificent mass, apparently trachytic from its resemblance to the Tarawera mountain, its face
for several hundred feet scarped and bare, and presenting
occasionally an appearance resembling a basaltic columnar
formation. This was Whakapunake, the last home, so
Maori tradition relates, of the moa on the East Coast. Before us lay a jumbled mass of mountain and vale, and in the
hollow beneath, a number of circular ponds, their edges
fringed with reeds and a small circle of clear water in their
centre, gave the impression that in former times they had
been "Ngawas" (hot springs) similar to those of Rotomahana. Away to the right were more and more ranges, one
mountain top, shaped something like a lion couchant, being
pointed out as Mangapohatu, the stronghold of the Uriwera,
a tribe still bitterly hostile at the time of my journey.

We passed the valley of ponds, and after some more riding,
stood on the summit of a spur leading down to a narrow

gorge, from the furthest end of which was rising a cloud of—
smoke? No: this was the spray of the Te Reinga falls. We
were now on one of the spots where Te Kooti was attacked
after his escape and landing from the Chatham Islands; on
this occasion the native allies executed a strategic movement
up the spur we were now about to descend, leaving the dozen
or so Europeans with them to shift for themselves; and it was
only by keeping a good countenance and shooting straight that
these managed to hold the enemy at bay and get away.

At the bottom of the spur we were in a beautiful little
valley, through which was rolling our old friend the Huangaroa, and presently we got into a thick scrub where
we had to cut our **way, the track** being completely
overgrown, so that it was getting dusk before we emerged
from it and stood at the junction of the Huangaroa and
Ruaketuri rivers, directly over the fall.

The two rivers meet at about two hundred yards from a
high range along the western flank of which the Ruaketuri
has been flowing, and which extends perpendicularly to the
course adopted by the united streams. Straight towards it
they flow, till, close to the foot of the range, their course is
arrested by a white **reef** barring their progress and damming
up their waters into a large pool. But not right across does
it extend; it stops short a few yards from the face of the
cliff on the right bank, and **through** the narrow opening
thus left the **whole body of** water rushes in a clear wave,
shooting some **ten feet** down to meet a precipitous cliff
which diverts it in a second fall to the left. Of these shoots
there are three, **in which the river** makes a quarter circle;
then, with one mighty plunge, it precipitates itself sideways
some ninety feet down into a yawning gulf, strikes the face of
the rock on the left bank, turns sharp round to the right,
and hurls itself through a chasm which it has cut sheer
through the range.

Standing on the limestone reef which arrests the rivers you cannot see the main fall ; to your right are the small shoots rushing down to it ; but directly before you is a straight gap some thirty yards in width and three hundred yards in length, an uncovered tunnel if you like, the sides of which are sheer rock, and cut down, as clean as if machinery had been employed, from a height equal to that on which you stand ; above the steep part the hill sides slope off and are covered with dense bush. Through this gulch the river roars down in many a swirl and wave and bound, sending up its spray to moisten the rich growth of ferns clothing the slopes under the heavy forest, tearing madly at the walls of rock which restrain it within bounds, and finally ending its wild career by subsiding suddenly into the quietest of demeanours, and finishing its headlong race in an open and placid pool. Right through the mountain it has cut a straight line, and the vista afforded of the calm lagoon at the further end of the chasm, fringed with low bush and gleaming in the sun, compared with the dark and gloomy glen through which the boiling torrent pours to attain a peaceful haven, forms a scene which, once beheld, can never be forgotten.

There are persons who having once gazed upon some grand natural feature, cannot stoop to the admiration of similar scenery on a smaller scale. I confess I am not one of these ; and it no more entered my head to make any invidious comparisons between Te Reinga and Schaffhausen, or any other cataract of European celebrity, than it would to turn up my nose at my daily joint because I have dined at the Trois Frères. The Reinga fall is simply a magnificent sight ; at least I thought it so on first acquaintance, and I know I shall think so again on my next visit. There is but one fault to be found with it ; only from one spot can the main fall be seen in its entirety, and that is from the mountain path on the left bank.

As in picnic-gully, so here the rock was full of fossils; the white reef running above the fall was one mass of shells deeply imbedded in it, and I naturally set to work with a tomahawk to dig up specimens, which we found could not be carried away : but, as before, I believe they were mostly identical with extant species.

We knocked up a "maemae" in a deserted *kainga*, the old posts of which came in handy for bivouac fires, and we slept soundly, notwithstanding the noise at hand.   Next morning, while getting my horse, I came upon a circular hollow strongly reminding me of the Rotorua pools ; it had the same wide-lipped inverted funnel shape, and it was not till after sundry prods with a stick that I felt reassured enough to trust myself at the bottom.   If this was not an extinct *ngawa*, it ought to be ; hardly a philosophical way to put it, perhaps ; but after all, not much worse than many a theory broached on extra scientific grounds.

The river having made a way through the range only for itself, we had to climb over the hill, and it was while on the path that we got our view of the big shoot, but even then the spray was so heavy that much could not be seen.   The descent brought us down to the margin of the pool which receives the waters as they come out, and I had a scramble up into the chasm.   For there is gulch within gulch ; there is the main rift, which, when the waters are in fresh, is described as presenting a magnificent appearance ; and, in the centre of this, a smaller furrow has been scooped out, sufficient for the summer flow as we found it.

The lagoon itself was a charming little spot, so pretty and so soft-looking after the scenery we had just passed through ; and I thought it exactly the spot I would recommend as head-quarters for a pic-nic excursion to last for a fortnight, the whole of which time could be very profitably taken up by explorations.   (I mean myself to spend a holy-

day there some time or another.)   In the first place, on the
further side of the river there are caves the floor of which
is covered by a stalagmitic deposit; these it would be most
interesting to trench thoroughly in search of fossils and
bones; there is the valley of the Ruaketuri, with its wild
scenery; and lastly there is Whakapunake, with its subter-
ranean river, its caves, and its grottoes in the face of the
cliffs.   In short there is plenty to do and to be seen.

Three or four more climbs and descents brought us to the
Wairoa plains, a fine level bit of country, well grassed, and
apparently good land, but deserted.   However there was
not much wonder at this, for the Uriwera were not far off,
and it was not so very long before this that Te Kooti
had come down and done a deal of mischief at the very
military township.

At a prettily situated Maori *kainga* (once occupied by
rank Hau-Haus) we forded the Mangapoiki, flowing rather
more peaceably than it did in the Reinga chasm, and a few
miles canter brought us to Te Kapu, the military township.
Te Wairoa, the district, takes its name from the river
which, formed by the waters issuing from the lofty ranges
surrounding the plain, rolls down in a fine and broad stream
to the sea, but is spoiled for navigation by a very ugly bar.

The position of the settlement is so far disadvantageous,
especially as the road to the nearest port, Napier, is
decidedly bad; but there is abundance of good country,
plenty of room for farms and small runs, and the Reinga
track is now being surveyed with a view to the construction
of a road connecting Wairoa with Poverty Bay.

CHAPTER XII.

WAIKARIMOANA.

It was on a subsequent visit to Wairoa that I was enabled to get up to the Waikarimoana Lake.

From the successes achieved in Wairoa in 1865 by the colonial forces, and by the friendly Ngatiporou under Major Ropata, may be dated the first break down of Hau-Hauism. Beaten in the open, and in their pas, the Hau-Haus retired on their inland sea and mountainous regions, not without suffering another heavy defeat on the way. But still for a long time the shores of Waikarimoana were closed to Europeans, and an expedition which reached them in 1869, had to return unproductive of good. The surrender of the Uriwera has however altered this state of things, and we possess now a small post of Constabulary on the very margin of the "Star Lake," as it is called on account of its numerous bays.

It is an easy ride from Te Kapu to Waikarimoana; but still we started at day-break for comfort's sake. There is no time for travelling on a hot summer's day in New Zealand like the very early morning; the air is so deliciously balmy, there is no oppressiveness, and everything looks so cool and refreshed; besides this, one's horse benefits by a rest during the mid-day heat.

Our path lay up a valley fringed with low hills and containing an extent of country able to support a large population; as usual, this was military settlers' land, and barren-

2 L

ness reigned supreme, with however one exception; the
track was lined with wild strawberry plants, not yet ripe.
Further on, near Waikarimoana, we passed through a perfect
grove of raspberries, and at Onepoto we learnt that quanti-
ties of the fruit existed on the other side of the Lake.   As
no mission stations have ever been founded so far, the presence
of these fruits in such wild spots is a puzzle.

Through the valley ran the Waikare-Taheke river, one of
the affluents of the Wairoa; this we had to ford five or six
times, getting into the hills after the last crossing.   Half-
way up the first rise we came upon a waterfall of really much
more respectable appearance than many which are visited at
home as curiosities; here we just pulled up for a look, lit a
pipe, and resumed our journey over a series of mild ascents
and descents till at length we reached a pretty high ridge
from which was caught a sight of the Waikare-Taheke.   To
the right of the path there was a tolerably steep gully, down
which, in 1869, one of the boats belonging to the expedition
took it into its head to slide.   The intention then was to move
a force across the lake, and large whaleboats were tugged
up on trucks, the only accident occurring at this spot.
The labour of getting the runaway up several hundred feet
of a steep ferny hill side may be conceived.

It may be laid down as an axiom that whenever the
tourist in New Zealand arrives at a hill christened " Gentle
Annie" he may prepare himself for a breather; there was
no exception to the rule as far as concerned the " Gentle
Annie" of Waikarimoana, and it was uncommonly hot work
getting up to the top.   However, there was a good view, so
that was an excuse for a halt.   Long before reaching this a
peculiar break in the hills had been pointed out as the site
of the Lake, and we had it now just before us; a wooded
high range stretched away in front, of a sudden ending
in a cliff looking for all the world like a sea-washed head-

land, and then sloped steeply down for several hundred feet, sinking into a low ridge which shortly rose up once more into a chain of hills extending to the eastward.

Far down below and to the right was still the Waikare-Taheke valley, the river running through it at a furious rate ; and, on the ridge connecting the two ranges, we could perceive a couple of small houses shewing the position of Onepoto. Even this saddle was high enough to prevent our getting a glimpse of the lake.

It had been hot work climbing up the hill ; it was worse going down, for this face was composed entirely of loose, deep pumice sand, into which we sank well over the ankles, creating at every step a cloud of stifling dust. To the right we could hear the hollow thundering of a waterfall, and from one point we managed to catch a glimpse of a mass of water pouring over a ledge, but we were far too hot and thirsty to go out of our way to see anything, and so we tramped on still downwards till we reached the brink of the river which lower down formed the cascade. From this we were about a mile from the lake, and strange to say, it was all up-hill work again, first past a "spinney" of raspberries, then along a glen strewn with boulders. These lay around in numbers, and of all sizes, from the round stone resembling a cannon ball to monoliths fit to compare with the slabs of the Temple of the Sun at Baalbec. I must say I should like an explana tion of how they came in this particular spot, whether they were shot out of some ancient volcano, or flung down from the heights when the break was made in the hills at One-poto, whether by an earthquake, by volcanic agency, or by an outburst of the lake. We found afterwards that similar masses lay imbedded in the soil at the spot where the camp is formed, and gave much trouble during the erection of the redoubt.

Presently we rounded a corner, cantered up a slight ascent

with a hollow to our left containing a couple of ponds, and saw before us a narrow ridge on which was situated the Constabulary post : we walked across the tiny parade ground, and at our feet lay Waikarimoana. The first feeling on looking at it from this point is one of disappointment ; there is no extent of water to be seen, and the view is shut up by hills all around.   To see the lake properly, there is but one way, and that is to climb up Panekiri hill, the quasi-headland mentioned above.   From this summit the shape of the lake is apparent ; it is a kind of irregular star with arms running up inland in all directions, in one case two capes projecting towards each other so far as to leave between them but a narrow strait, the entrance to another expanse of water, called Te Wairau. Various spots of interest were taken in at almost one glance ; there was the narrow arm of the lake which Te Kooti and his hard pressed followers swam on horseback to escape the pursuit of the flying columns on his track ; opposite was the *kainga* where, in 1869, he had lived securely and quietly, undisturbed by the preparations for attack from our side ; the lofty and chaotic masses of mountains at the back of this were the home of the Uriwera ; extending away to the right was the Aniwaniwa branch, at the head of which the river of the same name tumbles over a lofty cliff ; just below a point jutting out to the right of Onepoto lay sunk in several fathoms of water the boats brought up with so much trouble ; and beyond this again was a veritable whirlpool in which the water could be seen to go round and round, exactly as it does in a bath when the stop is lifted.

With such a view in sight the tourist feels no longer the sense of disappointment ; he has before him a glassy inland sea enclosed around by high cliffs and peaks, and rendered attractive by the wildness of the scene.   For, with the exception of a few patches of Maori cultivations, the country all about is just as it was left by Dame Nature when in her last throes she dug out and filled this huge crater, and piled up the mountains surrounding it.

But few landing places exist on Waikarimoana : the sides of the cliffs are precipitous, and woe betide the boat or canoe well out in the centre when the wild, fierce mountain blasts rush screaming down one of the numerous arms, and raise in a few minutes waves against which no resistance is of avail. Native tradition has numerous tales of canoes never heard of after leaving the shore.

A few young men of the Uriwera were at the post on our arrival, having come over from the other side, and once more I remarked the difference of features which exists, not only between them and the coast natives, but even among each other. The majority are much darker than the usual type of the Maori, and are distinguished by flat noses and blubber lips, in many cases as marked as those of the negro. Others, on the contrary, have a perfect Jewish cast of countenance, so remarkably developed as to attract immediate attention, and are very handsome specimens of manhood. Mountain and bush bred, they are as active as cats, and it is marvellous to see an Uriwera, laden with his swag and rifle, literally run up and down hills covered with a dense overgrowth through which Europeans have to move at a snail's pace. Their legs would make splendid models, and their feet, as a rule, are very large. I remember on one occasion, after a party of them had attacked a redoubt at Opotiki and been beaten off, seeing a friendly native gazing with admiration on one of the slain they had left behind. The body was that of a well proportioned young man, but it was the enormous feet which rivetted my friend's attention. "Ah" he said, "what feet for walking! How I should walk, if I had feet like that!"

The great lion of Waikarimoana is the source of the Waikare-Taheke; and notwithstanding that I had heard some reports about it, I was still greatly puzzled as to where on earth the river came from. When on Gentle Annie we had seen it below us careering along the valley in a series of foaming rapids and in a good wholesome torrent-like fashion ; yet the fall of the ground did not appear to be at all so steep as to justify such behaviour; and thus, great was our curiosity.

Leaving the camp and following the narrow ridge to the right where it commenced once more to ascend, a short walk brought us into a gully from which we emerged on to the shore of the lake, consisting of a reef about six or seven yards wide running along the foot of the cliffs which here formed a small bay. Some fifty yards further on, the reef ceased, and a promontory with steep sides jutted out into the lake. It was at this point that the whirlpool existed : but no trace of it was now seen, for a westerly wind had sprung up, and the short chopping sea hid the swirl of the water. Walking along the reef we had thus the lake to our left, cliffs to our right. Suddenly a cleft appeared in the latter, and in this our guide and host disappeared. It was certainly a very curious place, to say the least of it ; the side of the reef went down straight for about twelve or fifteen feet below us till it touched the bottom of a narrow ravine littered with a confused mass of boulders. This was evidently the bed of a mountain torrent, but whence came the water which had hollowed it out? A glance behind told us : there was only a space of some six or seven yards of rock between the edge of the lake and the cliff, and we could now understand why it was that the Wairoa always freshed so quickly in westerly weather. The wind from that quarter banks up the lake towards this, its only visible outlet, the barrier of reef is soon surmounted, and down pours the accumulation heaped up in this little corner to come down the Waikare-Taheke valley in a wave and to fall

suddenly into the Wairoa river. However there was no
overflow this day, and yet the Waikare-Taheke was, we
knew, running merrily, so there was still some mystery.
We let ourselves down into the gully which sloped away at
a fair incline, and in which the power of water was exemplified with a vengeance; great holes were scooped out of
the sides, masses of rock lay across each other at all sorts of
angles, all worn perfectly smooth; and where the stony
bottom had presented the least hardness of surface, it was
grooved into furrows with jagged edges. As we went down,
each moment increasing our distance below the level of the
lake, a hoarse and dull roar was heard ahead reverberating
along the precipitous walls of the cañon and re-echoing
in the deep indentations in its side; it became gradually
louder and louder; and, after walking some two hundred
yards we came to a series of huge boulders, carpeted with a
green and slippery moss. Warned to be cautious, we crept
carefully over these, and, looking over the hugest of the lot,
saw the source of the Waikare-Taheke where, a few feet
below us, the river leaped out of the ground and poured
down in a cataract. The main body of the water came from
under our friendly boulder; but, on all sides, tiny streamlets
issued from nooks and corners, from cracks in the rock, and
from among the roots of the trees which formed a dense
shade overhead. It was a beautiful sight; a living picture
of the water gushing out of the rock at the bidding of
Moses.

We went round to the left and, after a bit of a scramble
and some careful walking over moss-covered rocks around
whose bases murmured numberless rills each hastening to
contribute its share to the river, we got to a detached
boulder situated about opposite the main shoot. The fall is
of no height, some ten or twelve feet, but the adjuncts to it
set it off to much advantage; it was fine to watch this mass

of water burst forth out of its prison and take its leap into
the free open air, the whiteness of the foam contrasting so
strongly with the black wall of cliffs, with the grey boulders
covered with light green moss, and with the sombre hue of
the foliage overhead.

The little streams around, winding in and out, looked
absurdly like so many water-babies who had for a time lost
their mother and were doing their best once more to find
her, clasp hold of the skirt of her garment and hurry off
with her in her mad gallop down hill ; and how they rippled
and murmured, and complained whenever a big stone crossed
their path and made them turn to one side or the other, or,
worst of all, go over it ; murmurs and complaints both
ceasing when the last happy rush incorporated them into
their noisy parent.

Verily that boulder was a seat for a contemplative mind ;
it was a spot where one ought to be alone, and where a busy
brain might weave fancy after fancy, and compose any
number of unreadable verses.

We made a guess at the origin of the cascade, and proved
right. The whirlpool pointed out to us communicates, it is
believed, by a funnel with underground passages, and these
in fine weather form the sole exit of the lake ; during
westerly winds, as I have before said, this is supplemented
by the waters driven over the reef.

In going back we learnt a little about what concentrated
wind can do. There was not much of it outside, as we
found out, but in the chasm it was howling down at a terrific
rate, blowing so hard that once or twice it was as much as
one could do to make way against it. While struggling up
it was almost impossible to resist a sort of doubt as to the
soundness of the reef ahead, and the awkward thought
would occur, " How if it gave way just now ?"

Looking at such a formation one can understand how have

originated some of the inundations, historical and pre-historical, which have left their marks so plainly on the face of the earth. Suppose an earthquake, or a few pounds of nitroglycerine judiciously applied to the eighteen or twenty-one feet of rock between the lake and the gully; there would at once be an opening through which would rush a body of water some sixty or seventy square miles in area, and fifteen or more feet in depth. Should such a catastrophe ever occur, there is no doubt that the bar of the Wairoa would disappear; but then the whole district would go as well.

By the time we stood again on the reef the waves had encroached upon it certainly a foot, a presage of what was certain to happen in case of a continuance of the westerly weather, and of this there seemed every chance; black clouds were gathering over the mountain tops, and nature's barometer pointed to " decidedly stormy."

Onepoto was a very pleasant place to spend a week at in fine weather; we could have sailed, or rather paddled, round the lake and poked about in and out of the various arms, seen the Aniwaniwa falls, &c.; but the prospect of a week's rain in this high region, with the certainty of being jammed by the rivers for a week more was not lively. So, warned by the ominous look of the skies we started off that same afternoon, and not a bit too soon. The next day it came down heavily; even at Te Kapu all communication with Wairoa was cut off by the swelling of an unbridged creek, and it was four or five days before we could start for Napier.

I once asked a native what sort of road it was from Napier to Wairoa; he described it simply by holding up one hand with the fingers outstretched and running the forefinger of the other hand up and down them, and we found his description correct. Lofty ranges, on the summit of which crops out a hard shelly conglomerate, and deep glens constitute the character of the country. On the first day's journey a pretty spot was passed where the Mohaka river has furrowed its way through a fairish sized plateau, preserving here the dangerous character it has acquired higher up on the Taupo road, and rendered additionally dangerous by the nature of the cliff, " Papa" rock.

Notwithstanding the nature of the country, the horse track is good, and a couple of days' riding brings a traveller from Wairoa to Napier without distress to his steed.

CHAPTER XIII.

Up the West Coast.

The reader who has good-naturedly followed me in my rambles about the East Coast must be by this time as tired of mountain scenery as I used to be after a continuous series of climbs ; on this trip I can assure him he will find only one hill over which to exercise his legs in imagination.

It was on a fine February morning that in company with some friends I started off in Cobb's coach from Wellington, and bowled along in comparative comfort on the smooth Hutt road ; the water was just ruffled by a gentle breeze which served to cool the temperature ; the hills enclosing the bay, and which render it an almost perfect lake, were sharply defined against the clear blue sky ; over the Hutt valley hung a morning mist, destined to speedy dissolution ; and the view northward was closed by the saddle-back of Rimu-taka, the hill of winds, which separates the Hutt from the Wairarapa plains. In our school-boy days we were taught on Virgil's authority that Eolus dwelt in a cave : had the poet lived in these times and visited New Zealand he would have made the God's habitat on the top of a hill, and that hill would have been Rimutaka.

At Ngahauranga, the road turns off to the left through a gap in the hills, skirts the margin of the harbour of Porirua on the West Coast, passes through the pretty defile of Horo-kiwi, and rises to the summit of Paikakariki, up which we had to take our only climb on this journey.

From this there was a fine view of both sea and land ; to the right ran a range of hills, and between them and the sea, as far as the eye could reach, stretched out a long, level strip of country, widening out as it extended northward ; to the left lay the sea with hardly a ripple on its glassy surface, while the island of Kapiti, only some fifteen miles off, exhibited a succession of tints, as the rays of the sun struck upon its dark rocks, brown fern, or green sward of grass.

The beaches on the East Coast used to appear dreary ; but they were broken every twenty miles or so by hills. Here we had to go seventy miles straight on end on the sand. At first the sensation was very pleasant ; the driver shook his reins, and away we went at full gallop over a beach so hard and firm that we seemed to glide ; there was no shaking, no perceptible motion ; it was delightful. Of course this pace could not last for ever ; and after we had done some fifteen miles it dawned upon us that the waves to the left very much resembled each other ; that the sand hills on the right exhibited but little variety, and that the beach ahead always presented the same appearance. In fact, as Mark Twain's friend observed, it was monotonous. There was a change however occasionally, and that was when we got into deep sand, and had to work our passage by walking at the coachman's request. I don't know which of the two was the most tiresome.

On we went over the everlasting sand, the only variety being an occasional turn inland to change horses or pick up mails ; thus we stopped at Waikanae and Otaki, two native *kaingas* ; the latter, the great place of the Church missionaries in New Zealand where, whatever other results may have been achieved, the morality of the resident Maories, according to common report, has not been much improved. At last, weary and stiff, we were not sorry to pull up for the night at Foxton.

Day-break saw us off once more over the same kind of monotonous beach which made one quite sympathise with the Walrus in " Alice through the looking-glass," when he expressed a wish to see a clean sweep made of the sea-side sand ; and near the Rangitikei river, we joyfully turned inland for good.

With sand-hills circumscribing the view it is not possible to give any account of what lies beyond them, but on rising up the plateau on the right bank of the Rangitikei we could see that, inland of those we had had on our right hand, there was a fine expanse of country, for the most part awaiting occupants. It is hoped these will ere long make their appearance, whether under the auspices of the English emigration company which has purchased a large tract of land about here, or under those of the province which is disposing by auction of portions of its landed estate, and is also bent on adding to it by purchase from native owners with a view to attracting population.

We skirted the Rangitikei for some miles, turned again northwards along a good road traversing land under cultivation, passed through Marton and the pretty hollow of Turakina, and on the evening of the second day from Wellington clattered over the really fine bridge which now spans the Whanganui river.

Were it not for the sand hills which bound one end of the town and which rise up in its centre, Whanganui would be a pretty place. It lies in the hollow scooped out by the river of the same name, whose alluvial deposit has produced a marvellous loam ; a walking stick can be pushed down to its full extent by the merest pressure, and it need scarcely be said that such soil will grow anything. The town is neatly laid out at right angles, and is embellished, or disfigured (whichever is the proper term), by a statue to the memory of the loyal natives who fell at the fight of Moutoa, and by a Court House in the Novo-Zealandico style of architecture.

The Whanganui river takes its rise in the interior ranges close to the foot of Ruapehu, and for miles traverses a broken and difficult country which stands to the West Coast in the same relation that the glens of the Uriwera do to the East Coast. Precipitous cliffs and numerous rapids, as many as 180 of the latter having been counted, are the characteristics of the upper portion of the river, while lower down it passes through a less rugged region. It was on its banks at Pipiriki that a hostile force besieged and reduced to great straits a small European garrison; and on Moutoa, an island in its bed, a fierce conflict took place between friendly and inimical natives in which the former were victorious. The Maori population on its shores cannot now be estimated at above 1500 or 2000 souls; those on the upper waters having only lately abandoned their enmity to the Europeans, while those of the lower part have for years proved true and staunch friends, one of their highest chiefs, Major Kepa te Rangihiwinui, being one of the loyal natives to whom Her Majesty has presented a sword of honour.

During our stay at Whanganui much discussion was afoot respecting an alleged gold-field at Tuhua, a region about the sources of the Whanganui, and some chiefs of note were in town about it. One of them, Te Mamaku, was a fine specimen of the Maori of old times. He must have been an immensely powerful man in his youth, and now he was as upright as a dart. When young, few warriors had distinguished themselves above him; and that was a time when any one who cared at all about fighting need not go very far to enjoy the pastime. If there was nothing going on between the Europeans and the natives, the latter could always get up a very fair excuse for coming to blows among themselves; for instance, a war broke out once between two sections of the Ngapuhi, north of Auckland, caused simply by one young girl cursing the tribe of another while both were bathing. In many encounters, both intertribal and against the early settlers, Te Mamaku had been engaged; but now in his old age thoughts of peace and quiet had stolen upon him, and the proposed exploration of Tuhua with a view to ascertaining its auriferous qualities met with his approval in his capacity as one of the leading chiefs of the district. According to the accounts of his followers, the field is rich; but how far their statements are to be relied upon remains yet to be proved.

From Whanganui we started in a light trap, and at the outskirts of the town a rise took us out of the valley on to the plateau through which the river has ploughed its way.

Presently we passed Westmere and its ponds, and getting on to a good metalled road, we drove along with well-kept paddocks to either hand. A short distance ahead was a bluff overlooking the Kai Iwi river, and nearly down to this came the bush, formerly the haunt of Tito Kowaru's men when in rebellion. Away to the left lay the sea, and to the right numerous comfortable houses had taken the place of those burnt by the Hau-Haus in 1869, or marked the spots where fresh settlers had set up their lares and penates.

The characteristics of the coast commenced now to shew themselves. It is a strip of magnificent land averaging about six to eight miles in width from the sand-hills on the beach to the bush inland, and we could now perceive that this latter was really very broken country, though none of the hills compared in height with those of the Uriwera. Issuing from the bush, a number of streams ran down to the sea furrowing the plain in their course, and forming most picturesque ravines, some of them being of a decent depth; the rivers fresh rapidly and considerably, but we did not hear of their overflowing the banks. One element in the scenery

is not to be passed over. Soon after reaching the plateau
overlooking Whanganui a huge white mass far inland forcibly
arrested the attention ; we knew it at once ; it was our old
friend Ruapehu. But right ahead also was another mountain, and of this the eye never tired. There is only one other
that I have seen in the world which can compare with it in
beauty of outline, although at the. same time exceeding it
far in size, and that is the " Finster Aarhorn" in the Ber-
nese Oberland. But the Finster forms part of a chain,
while Mount Egmont is solitary in its grandeur. Seen from
where we were, it sweeps magnificently up from both sea
and land, the outline as clear and sharp against the sky as
the edge of a knife ; gradually it rises, shooting up a bare
mass from the dense forest which clothes the base, and ending in a peak never quite free of snow. When we saw it this
time, this only lay in streaks in the ravines grooved along
the flanks, but in winter it extends far down. At a later
period in the journey a light mist rose about half-way up
the cone, yet not dense enough to prevent the eye from trac-
ing the graceful contour, while a cumulus cloud hovered
around the summit, keeping on the northern side, and
presenting the appearance of a huge volume of white smoke
rolling lazily out of the mouth of an active volcano. It was
a glorious sight.

Maori tradition relates that Taranaki, as the natives call
Mount Egmont, once lived with his brother Ruapehu and
his sister Tongariro in comfortable family union on the
shores of Taupo. Dissensions will occur, even in the best
regulated families ; and in that which ensued in this remarkable household, Tongariro and Ruapehu sided together
against Egmont ; so the latter, in disgust at their behaviour,
started off determined to commit suicide by throwing himself into the sea. He did not time his journey very well,
and so it was getting dark before he reached the coast ; such

was his eagerness however, that he went blundering on, and,
in trying to get past between two hills, which now appear to
belong to him, he stuck fast. There he now remains, with the
whole country to himself and no one to bother him, except
when some sacrilegious European insists upon climbing up to
see what his head is made of.

We travelled along a capital road, such a one as Waikato settlers would give anything to have between Mercer
and Ngaruawahia, which dipped into ravines through which
flowed streams, running at present with only a scanty supply
of water; then at other times rose by sidings cut through
bits of bush and following the windings of picturesquely
wooded gullies, and again ran straight along level plateaux.
On one of these we passed by Taurangaika, the stronghold
for a length of time occupied by Tito Kowaru and his
Hau-Hau band, whence his men, mounted as well as on foot,
were wont to sally and roam unmolested over ground which
now affords pasture in safety to flocks of sheep and herds of
fat cattle. We were now going through country which had
known desolation; abandoned to the enemy in 1869 by the
concentration of the colonial troops on the line of the Kai
Iwi river (which we crossed a few miles out of Whanganui),
not a European could ride about it and live; and soon after
the retreat of the forces the elated natives pushed their
parties well ahead, and nightly fires seen from the camps
denoted the destruction of homestead after homestead; nay,
alarms were frequent in the town itself. Communication
with the Patea district was cut off, and no convoy to that
post could pass without a strong escort. It was while on
one of these that I saw what effect a long range bullet may
have. We had just been relieved as skirmishers and were
trudging down to Nukumaru camp for dinner through a
small gully, when one of my men suddenly fell; we could
not imagine him wounded, for besides that we were under

2 D

shelter, the nearest Hau-Haus could not have been less than
a mile off. Yet the poor fellow was hit by a stray bullet,
fired at a high angle, which had dropped down on his skull.
Times were now changed ; the very pa, which had been a
model of Maori fortification, was a mere heap of earth undis-
tinguishable by a stranger ; an hotel stood close to where
our men used to have to keep well under shelter during the
attack on the pa, and all sign of strife had disappeared.

Not far to the left, by some lagoons, was Nukumaru, a
spot where General Cameron's camp was boldly attacked by
a small party of King natives, who indeed got pretty close
to the General's tent and did a considerable deal of mischief
before being driven back.

Not long after leaving Taurangaika a fairish descent brought
us to the bank of the Waitotara river, crossed here by a punt;
and, a little way up stream, a telegraph post on a bluff denoted
the *locale* of the Wereroa redoubt taken, when a hostile
pa, by Sir George Grey and the colonials, afterwards held by
a party of Whanganui lads against Tito's men, and now
merely a crumbling mass of earth.

Punted across, we found, situated not far from the spot
where some of our men were tomahawked in 1869 while
gathering fruit in a peach-grove, one of the most comfortable
little hotels that it has been my lot to come across while
travelling in the North Island, and we also picked up an
incident of Maori character. While at luncheon we saw a
very respectably dressed native about the place, and learned
about him the following particulars. He had been in
rebellion and had surrendered ; but on giving himself up
he found that all his ancestral land had been confiscated,
and that there was none of it left for him to occupy : this
so preyed upon him that he quite lost his mind and wandered
about the mountains, a perfect lunatic. Now, had he
happened to come across a European while in this state,

there was every chance he would have thought it his duty to take "utu" and slay his man, and thence might have arisen further bloodshed. But his state became known to the landlord, who had bought from the Government part of the unfortunate fellow's original estate : he sent a party of natives after him, got him in, gave him a bit of the land which he coveted ; and the man is now clothed and in his right mind, living with his people in perfect content at a little *kainga* they have built not far down the stream. A stray fact or two like this gives an insight into Maori ideas so far as the love of the soil is concerned, and shews the intensely passionate feeling with which the native clings to his ancestral patrimony.

The Waitotara river forms the southern boundary of the territory which, confiscated in 1864 for the rebellion of its owners, has yet only been partially taken possession of. Its original owners clung to the soil ; driven from their habitations on the coast they took refuge on the outskirts of the bush, and, as they were pressed, retreated further and further into its recesses, only to issue out again on every possible opportunity, till in 1868, they achieved success so far as to push us back almost to Whanganui itself. Of course this did not last, and the West Coast tribes were once more driven from place to place, till their confederacy was broken up, and only a small remnant was left which has taken up its abode on the flanks of Mount Egmont, and contents itself with preserving a peaceful though sullen attitude. Notwithstanding this, these very natives have been found willing to take work, and they have by their labour assisted in making the road skirting the coast which forms the highway from Whanganui to Taranaki.

The whole of the open land extending from the Waitotara to New Plymouth has been a battle-field on which Imperial and Colonial soldiers have time after time met, both in attack and defence, a foe whom they soon learned not to despise : almost every mile of road brings the traveller to the scene of some ambush or skirmish ; and at frequent intervals are pointed out spots memorable for genuine successes on our part, for doubtful victories, or for palpable defeats.

After leaving the Waitotara hotel there was not much sign of cultivation till we got to Wairoa, but here was found a military township with the best of all signs, a redoubt and blockhouse tumbling to pieces, and a new church built opposite to them. And this was close to the bush out of which in 1868 our men were followed out into the open by the Hau-Haus who had inflicted on us a heavy defeat at our attack on their pa at Moturoa ; now the only distinguishable sign of warfare was the " ping, ping" to be heard to the left where the district volunteers were competing for prizes.

From Wairoa it is no great distance to the Whenuakura, a nasty, deep-banked, heavy-freshing stream, presently to be bridged; and after being punted across, we got upon a bit of picked land, which has since our visit been sold by Government and has realised prices which prove its value.

It was quite refreshing, after passing over such large tracts on the East Coast all locked up and utterly useless at present, to find at last a quantity of land ready for the market, of such quality and situation as to ensure the formation of a prosperous settlement.

Patea was our *kainga moe*[*] that night, and we had here an exemplification of the wisdom of military engineers who, in despite of the Biblical aphorism, did found their town upon a sand-hill ; and this in a region which is evidently a favourite of the winds. The settlers have moved the township higher up, and no wonder ; for the sand storms used to be something dreadful, and a general grittiness was wont to pervade everything one ate, drank or smelt. The Patea is

---

[*] Kainga moe—sleeping place.

a fair sized river, but possesses a peculiarly nasty bar, the channel making a bend right among the breakers; possibly this may be amended, and the mouth of the river has been surveyed with a view to future dredging and improvement of the entrance.

The township now occupies the position of the old camp, and, before starting the next morning, I strolled up a small rise on which, behind parapets, used to stand my quarters. From this a fair view was obtained for a good many miles of the inland country rising gradually up to the edge of the bush, and constant used to be the watch for fires or any signs betokening the presence of the enemy who could move up or down the coast, sheltered by the forest from our observation, issue out secretly at any point and lay ambuscades for convoys or chance travellers. For some short distance after leaving Carlyle—as the place is called—the soil is sandy and poor, but about Kakaramea (another redoubt in ruins) it once more resumes its fertile character, and this it keeps for miles and miles. There is rich land lying here in a state of nature, calculated to maintain a population of thousands; and, that it will do so eventually, there can be no doubt; the climate is good, there is abundance of water, the bush is close at hand, the soil I have already spoken of, and the scenery is glorious; for we are getting nearer and nearer to Egmont, and still the mountain preserves the same regular and sublime outline; the road is really capital, and the bridges thrown across the streams which flow through the picturesque ravines grooved into the flat are substantial.

In the cuttings down to the Manawapou and Tangahoe rivers can be seen slender streaks of lignite, possible indications of a rumoured coal bed in the interior; but of this latter part of the country there is but little known, except that it is heavily bushed and very rugged in parts, while

portions exist of an undulating character which will at some
future day be eagerly taken up for settlement.

Some twenty miles from Patea we came to the small township of Hawera. All along we had been pleased with the
nature of the country, but here we could not help agreeing
with two intending settlers on the look-out for land whom
we had met off and on while travelling up—"By George,"
said one of them "this is the place for me." And he spoke
with good reason. A native I met at Hawera informed me
that in former days he had known ten successive crops of
wheat taken off the same spot of ground. Not far from
Hawera are situated extensive reservations made for the
returned rebels of the West Coast. One of the *hapus*
(sub-tribe)—the Pakakohe—became prisoners almost to
a man, were tried, and performed their sentence in Dunedin
jail. It was a pretty salutary punishment; they were
pardoned at the end of a couple of years, and returned
to their relations in splendid condition, with the advantage
of having picked up a fair share of English and learned
discipline. Some of the reserves made for them they have
leased to Europeans, and on others they have established
themselves, setting to work in a way which proves their
belief in the old Maori proverb, *Ehara te toa taua, he toa
pahekeheke; tena ko te toa mahi kai, ekore e paheke.* [He who
is strong in war is likely to slip; but he who is strong in
cultivating, he will not slip.] The example they afford
to their still discontented relatives some miles further
north will probably have a salutary effect.

About four miles from Hawera lies the frontier constabulary station of Waihi; a really well planned and splendidly
built stockade which it would puzzle a European force to
capture without artillery; for it combines with our views of
fortification all the ingenious ideas introduced in defence by
the Maori, who has proved himself to be no mean engineer.

Within sight from the elevated watchtower situated at one
of the angles of the stockade is the old redoubt of Turu-
turu-mokai, where poor Ross was surprised in 1868 and
killed with most of his people, and where some three or
four men resolutely held one angle against all that the
natives could do until relief came. Now one of them was
occupying in perfect tranquillity a farm close by the scene of
his exploit, and around him population was gradually creeping up and fencing in old sites of strife and bloodshed; in
short, security had replaced danger.

It was from Waihi that General Chute, and subsequently
a colonial force also, started for a march to Taranaki through
the dense bush clothing the eastern base of the mountain.
Taking pack horses &c. with him, the General had a good
deal of difficulty in getting through in about nine days ; the
more lightly equipped colonials, carrying all their baggage
themselves, managed it in four days, during which not a
single clearing was found. As in other parts of the Island,
so here roads are replacing the old bush tracks which used to
form the only means of communication ; and similarly as on
the East Coast former rebels are to be found industriously
employed on road-works, so here also the very tribes who
fought against us are employed in cutting a track through the
forest at the back of the mountain ; in reality they are com-
pleting what was begun some forty years ago, at the instigation of Europeans, by the grandfather of the chief whose
tribe is engaged in the work. The advantage of such a line
to the West Coast is obvious ; it shortens by forty miles the
distance between Waihi and the Waitara river, runs over
level country clad with bush which, though thick, is of a
nature to be easily cleared, and passes over very rich soil.
Some day an open plain will exist where nought but forest is
now to be found, and the whistle of the engine will replace the
groanings and creakings of branches bending before the gale,

The first northward river met after leaving Hawera possesses a name euphonious enough when issuing from a native's mouth, but barbarously harsh as it used to be pronounced by the British soldier who sounded the "g" hard: in Waingongoro, 'snoring water,' the "ng" is nasal.

Beyond this, settlement has not yet extended and a large expanse of country exists, all of it splendid land, stretching as far as the Hangatahua river, over which the progress of colonization is evinced by only two indications, the high road, and the small township of Opunake.   Once across the Hangatahua the traveller finds himself again in civilised regions.

F I N I S.